BUYING CUSTOMERS

Other Books By Bradley J. Sugars

The Business Coach

Instant Advertising

Instant Cashflow

Instant Leads

Instant Profit

Instant Promotions

Instant Referrals

Instant Repeat Business

Instant Sales

Instant Systems

Instant Team Building

Successful Franchising

Billionaire in Training

The Real Estate Coach

BUYING
CUSTOMERS

Revolutionary new rules for you to get more
customers with far less money.

Bradley J. Sugars

Printed in the United States of America
First Printing: March 2012

Library of Congress Control Number: 2012934801
13-digit ISBN: 978-0-692-01721-0

For additional information, visit:

Bradsugars.com

Contents

Introduction...3

1) The Five Ways to Profit...8

2) Allowable Acquisition Costs..23

3) Conversion Rates...32

4) What is Lifetime Value?...54

5) The Principles of Lifetime Value....................................75

6) Ways to Boost Lifetime Value..89

7) Getting Their Attention..120

8) Building Your Team...136

9) Strategies for Lead Generation....................................151

10) Strategies for Conversion Rates.................................187

11) Buying Customers Conclusion....................................210

Glossary..214

To all my customers ... you make it all worthwhile ...

To all my team ... you make it all possible ...

Buying Customers Introduction

It's another quiet Saturday and the shop is virtually empty.

An occasional prospect comes through the door only to wander around aimlessly, picking up an occasional item.

They seem unsure of what they want or why they are even there.

"Can I help you?"

"No, just looking."

Just minutes later the prospect walks back out to the street, nothing bought, no connection made, probably never to be seen in that business again.

This is an all too common scenario for many businesses, around the world, whether they are retail, wholesale, service providers or distributors.

But what if you knew the next customer to come through the door was one you "bought" into your business ... for a specific offer, for a certain product and at a certain price?

What if you knew the chances were 1 in 3 that the person you "bought" would spend the next 5 years buying more products from you at ever higher price points?

What if you had some certainty that every dollar you spent on buying new customers had a chance to actually return you that dollar, and even $2.00, $3.00 or $4.00, or more, down the road?

Would you look at your efforts to buy new customers as an expense ... or as an investment?

In the ever-competitive and increasing "flat" world of business and communication, it's no longer viable to continue to spend resources chasing customers.

The old adage of "half my advertising budget is wasted, but I don't know which half, " just doesn't cut it anymore.

Chasing customers is the old way of doing business.

Traditional marketing is the old way of doing business.

Buying customers is the new way to run your business ...

My goal, and the purpose of this book, is to show you how to effectively turn your business into a "customer buying machine" ... one that:

• Buys a quality customer at a value price ...

• Keeps that customer coming back for more ... and

• Gives that customer all the reason in the world to tell others about your great product or service, your team and your company.

This book is for anyone who wants to discover a new mindset about what it really takes to run a successful and profitable business by using some simple, yet powerful strategies and shifts in thinking that will not only put you miles ahead of your competition, but is guaranteed to put extra dollars on your bottom-line, and, more importantly, in your pocket.

So if you want to know what it means to "buy" a customer, how to do it and why it can mean the difference between success and failure for your business … read on …

The lessons, strategies and tactics outlined here will certainly give you the tools and metrics you'll need to create a customer buying program for your own company.

At the same time, it will also give you the confidence and certainty you need to actually put your own customer buying program into practice.

So who is Buying Customers for?

It's for everyone and anyone in the world of business.

Of course, business owners can use this concept, but think about the marketing manager that is trying to do more with fewer resources.

Understanding the principles of Buying Customers can help set expenses and even justify budget expenditures.

If a marketing manager can prove the work they're doing is actually being done at a profit, wouldn't they be given more leeway in their job?

How about sales people who are out on the road? How much money, time, energy and other resources are they putting forth every day?

Probably more than they need to.

But if they understood how to buy customers profitably, they would be able to leverage their resources more effectively, in turn generating more leads, customers, sales and profits.

If you are in business, any kind of business, in virtually any role, you need to understand the concept of Buying Customers.

Once you do, you'll never view business the same way again.

What if you could go out and start investing dollars that would bring new customers to you at a guaranteed profit?

What if you started looking at each customer as a true asset?

What if you start thinking of them as a real investment?

That is why I wrote "Buying Customers."

If you bought a stock or invested in a company, wouldn't you expect to see a return?

Why wouldn't you expect the same from your customers?

How long would you continue to "throw money" at an asset that doesn't give you a return?

Not very long, I would say.

But businesses do this every day because they don't know how to buy customers.

This book will change all of that.

Start buying assets.

Going out and actually buying your customers is a lot like buying an asset, and in some cases like "value" investing.

You want to get the best customers possible at the lowest possible price, expecting that customer to spend repeatedly with you over the course of several years (or a "lifetime").

In fact, a new customer's "Lifetime Value" is one of the keys in determining exactly how much you want to "pay" to buy that customer.

We'll get into the mechanics of "Lifetime Value" later, as well as acquisition costs and lead generation, but first I wanted to show you just how and why the process of buying a customer is so powerful, and then how it relates to what I call the "5 Ways" to massive profits and results.

The whole aim of this book is to teach you how to buy a customer for less and get them to spend more and more with you.

Imagine you could buy a customer for $10 and they immediately spent enough to give you $20 profit. That's right: $10 out and $20 back.

At this rate, how many lots of $10 would you invest?

When you know how to buy customers, you know you can invest as many $10 lots as your resources and cashflow will allow.

Buying customers is a revolution in thinking.

It's no longer about making a profit on a piece of stock or service.

It's about making profit on each and every customer, because if you buy them at the right price, you will always make a profit.

Buy enough of them and you will have a thriving, growth business.

Chapter 1:

The Five Ways to Profit

It's time to change your perspective on marketing. In fact, it's time to change the way all marketing is done. It's time to start Buying Customers.

Too many businesses treat marketing as an expense, when in reality it's an investment.

They do this because they don't truly understand what marketing is and how they can use this knowledge to buy customers.

You see, there is no business without customers. You may have great products, but if no one is buying, how is this benefitting you?

And isn't your goal to have a business that serves you with profit and fun?

To have a business that flows with profits, you have to understand the layers that go into Buying Customers.

It's about generating leads, converting them to customers, knowing the likely amount they will spend with you and keeping your customers around for as long as possible, and repeatedly buying again and again.

By following these steps, any business will be profitable. The problem is too many businesses stop short.

They spend loads of money on advertising to get their "brand" out there and maybe bring prospects into their store, and when the potential customers get there, the business makes little to no effort to keep them coming back.

They get excited by the initial sale, not knowing that each sale may have lost them money.

If your marketing works like that, you aren't Buying Customers.

In fact, you're throwing away your hard earned money by not following through and making "Raving Fans" out of the new customers that come to your business.

Buying Customers is about profit per customer, not profit per hours or profit per item.

If you can measure your profit per customer, you can figure out how much to invest in your marketing so that it is at the very least break-even, and, ideally, you make a profit upon acquisition of a new customer.

Buying Customers is a change in mindset that incorporates these ideas into a strategy; a methodology that can make any business profitable.

So how do you begin the change in mindset to Buying Customers?

You have to change the way you view your business.

You have to see it as a profit making machine and your customers are the investment that bring the profits in.

For a lot of businesses, they consider ideas like profit per sale or profit per item, but how many businesses think about profit per customer?

Not enough.

Any business' stock-in-trade is their customers and if you could make each and every customer that buys from you profitable for your business, think about what that would mean.

In future chapters, we will be talking about many the factors you need to know to buy customers effectively, including the important numbers that go into a business.

Numbers are the language of business.

If you don't know every relevant number in your business, you're bound to slip up somewhere, and that slip could come in the way you buy customers, which could hamper the rest of your business.

So before we get into the nuts and bolts of Buying Customers, let's talk about the "5 Ways."

Just keep in mind that where Buying Customers is concerned, the first four drivers are what really matter.

The "5 Ways" is a fairly simple formula that shows you how to multiply your profit based on just five key "drivers" that exist in any business – including yours.

Buying customers keys on:

1) Generating leads
2) Converting those leads into customers
3) Getting those customers buying from you time and again
4) Average dollar sale

The fifth driver, profit margins, is the easiest for any business to change.

The ones that we'll focus on are, for most businesses, the most challenging and expensive to affect – for a lot of different reasons.

However, once you see how each of these drivers can literally explode your bottom-line, and once you discover the value of buying customers versus chasing them, you'll immediately see ways in your own company you can decrease the costs of your "buy" while increasing the quality and long-term value of your customer base.

So ... let's take a look at the Five Ways ...

First off, here's the "5 Ways" formula ...

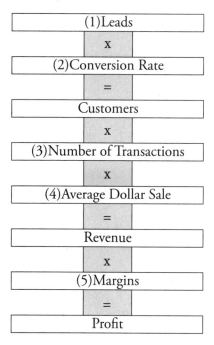

(1)Leads
x
(2)Conversion Rate
=
Customers
x
(3)Number of Transactions
x
(4)Average Dollar Sale
=
Revenue
x
(5)Margins
=
Profit

What does this really mean?

In the "old" way of thinking, profits can only be upped by focusing on the conventional accounting measure of:

Revenues - Expenses = Profits

What this means is you only have a few options to get more profit in your business.

You can either:

• *Increase revenues*
• *Decrease expenses*
• *Do a combination of both*

This is simple, but not very effective … especially if you've cut your expenses to the bone.

The "5 Ways" offers a different way of looking at the factors that drive profit, and also causes you to focus on growth in your company instead of cut-backs.

Not that you need to disregard expenses. That's silly and, as we will see, every cost in a business goes into the price of Buying Customers.

But no business has ever cut its way to great success … and the "5 Ways" will give you options for growth you never even knew you had before.

The "5 Ways" Step-by-Step

Let's go through each factor individually before we start to run some numbers …

1) Lead Generation

The first factor is lead generation, which is your number of leads or the total number of prospects that were in touch with your business over a given period of time.

Simply put, a lead is a person who has expressed interest in your product or service, but hasn't bought from you yet.

Many businesses confuse responses, or the number of potential buyers, with making a profit.

Don't make the same mistake.

Inquiries aren't customers ... and just because the phone is ringing, it doesn't mean the cash register is.

While Lead Generation is at the top of our formula, it's one of the most expensive factors to affect.

It's also the first driver most businesses focus on when they go off on a customer acquisition campaign.

We'll change that very soon ... but next we need to focus on the second way in the "5 Ways" ... Conversion Rates.

2) Conversion Rates

Leads are the first step, but unless you convert those leads into actual customers, you are getting nowhere.

Simply put, your Conversion Rate is the number of people that actually bought from you out of your total number of leads.

For example, if 10 people called your office today and you sold to only three of them, your conversion rate would be 30%.

One of the first things you can measure in your business is your conversion rate, which is key in leveraging the Buying Customers strategies.

If you don't know it, you're not alone.

Most marketing managers and salespeople don't have a realistic notion of how many leads they actually convert to customers.

Ignorance of this idea is no excuse, however, and now that you do know about it I challenge you to find out what it is for your business.

Here's a good exercise. Write down what you think your conversion rates are ... then actually go and measure them for two weeks.

When I ask the average business owner about their conversion rate, they invariably take a guess at the number, and typically that guess is unusually high.

Most people like to believe they convert at well over 50%, but the number is usually, at best, half whatever number they guess.

While nobody is ever happy to learn their numbers aren't what they think they are, knowing is actually a good thing, because you cannot manage what you do not measure.

In addition, if your conversion rates are really low, you have nowhere to go but up ... and that can have a huge, positive effect on your bottom-line.

3) Total Number of Transactions

Number three in the "5 Ways" is your total number of transactions.

Some customers may buy from you all the time, some once a week, some once a year, some just once and never again.

But at the start, let's call this the number of times they buy from you on average over the course of a year.

When you're starting to benchmark your own numbers, you may have to estimate this number. That's OK.

You'll soon see how to better determine and drive this number, as well as ways to increase this from your current – and new – customer base.

4) Average Value Dollar Sale

The next measurable variable to take into account is your average dollar sale, or the average amount your customers buy from you every time they purchase.

To start benchmarking, you'll again look for the average amount your customers spend per transaction.

For your initial purposes, just add up your total revenues/turnover and divide it by an estimated the number of transactions or sales.

5) Profit Margins

The final step (and easiest) way to start multiplying your profits is to increase your profit margins.

Your profit margin is simply the percentage of each and every sale that is profit.

In other words, if you sell something for $100 and your expenses are $70, your profit is $30.

If you divide your profit by your revenue ($30/$100) … you'll get your profit margin result.

How easy is it to raise your margins?

Many businesses fear raising prices because they don't want to upset their customers. But most customers won't even notice a small price increase and if you provide outstanding value and service, even if they notice, they won't mind.

So what if you simply raised your price points by 10%?

We'll see what affect this has in a minute … but this one factor is something you could do in your company tomorrow.

The "5 Ways" in practice.

Now that we've defined some terms, let's plug some numbers into the formula to see how our super-small example of a business is running now … and how it can run more profitably with just a small increase in each of the five drivers.

Our baseline:

Let's say you've run some numbers or estimates based on your current knowledge of your business and figured out you've got approximately 4,000 inquiries or active leads coming into your business on a yearly basis.

From that, you can convert 25% of those leads into actual sales.

That means you have a company with 1,000 active customers, and let's say that they each buy from you an average of 2 times per year, at an average sale value of $100.

That means you have a yearly revenues of $200,000.

With an average profit margin of 25%, your business generates a profit of $50,000.

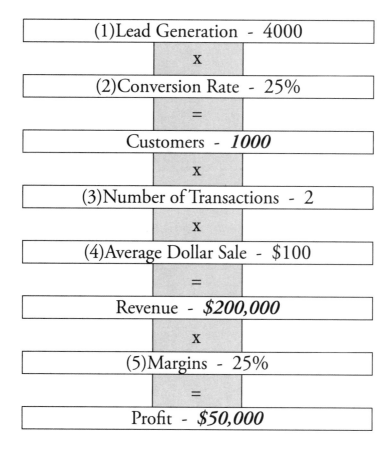

What would happen if we increased each of these 5 factors by just 10%?

Let's take a look ...

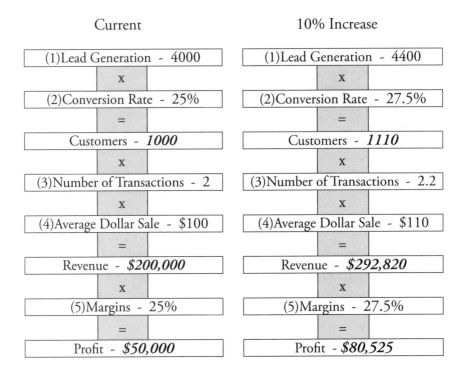

Interesting, huh?

Just a 10% increase in each factor creates a 46% increase in revenues and a massive 61% profit on your bottom line!

How can this be?

Because we are multiplying instead of simply adding or subtracting ... and when we do that we can get exponential leverage in your company.

If you think 10% looks good, see what profits look like when we double our numbers.

Now this may take several years, but you have to start somewhere.

(1)Lead Generation - 4000	(1)Lead Generation - 8000
x	x
(2)Conversion Rate - 25%	(2)Conversion Rate - 50%
=	=
Customers - *1000*	Customers - *2000*
x	x
(3)Number of Transactions - 2	(3)Number of Transactions - 4
x	x
(4)Average Dollar Sale - $100	(4)Average Dollar Sale - $200
=	=
Revenue - *$200,000*	Revenue - *$3,200,000*
x	x
(5)Margins - 25%	(5)Margins - 50%
=	=
Profit - *$50,000*	Profit - *$1,600,000*

Hopefully, these numbers start to show you the incredible value of investing resources into Buying Customers and in the potential that already exists in your company.

What the "5 Ways" Can Teach You About Buying Your Own Customers

How much you invest in buying your customers depends in large part on what type of business you are.

Businesses that focus on professional services may be able to rely on referrals for leads, although their number of transactions may not be as high as a retailer.

Then again, the average value sale of those companies may be significantly higher.

For retailers, the cost of lead generation may be high, but can be lowered, and depending on the niche, may generate high repeat business at a lower average sale, or lower repeat business at a higher average sale.

The "5 Ways" can help you find what the numbers are and what they can be for your company, so spend some time and do some calculations to see how your business fits into the model.

Now, we can work through what, for our purposes, are the key drivers for Buying Customers, namely lead generation, conversion rates and number of transactions and average dollar sale.

And, we can start to work out not only what you are willing to pay for a new customer, but what your numbers will allow you to pay to buy a new customer, at a price that will produce a profit for you and your business.

To learn more about the "5 Ways" be sure to visit actioncoach.com. If you want to download the "5 Ways" mobile app, go to iTunes and search "Brad Sugars + 5 Ways"

Chapter Review – "9 to Grow On"

1) Most people only see two ways to getting to a bottom-line profit, based on the formula:

   Revenues – Expenses = Profit

2) As a result, conventional business models and advice only focus on "growing the top line" or "cutting expenses" to get more profit

3) The "5 Ways" presents an alternative way to not only grow – but multiply profits

4) The "5 Ways" exists in every business on the planet (including your own)

5) Populating the "5 Ways" with your own numbers and working through them is the best way to see the multiplying power of the formula

6) The easiest and quickest way to improve your business with the "5 Ways" is to "start at the bottom" and "work your way up."

7) Profit margins and price points can easily be upped in most businesses by at least 10%

8) Lead Generation is the most expensive and hardest factor to improve, yet it's also the one factor most businesses target first.

9) That's why it's so important to know your numbers before you rush out and start buying customers.

3 Things to DO after your Review:

1) Look at your own business in terms of the "5 Ways." Copy the formula and work out your own business model in terms of the "5 Ways."

2) The easiest way to start the multiplication factor of the "5 Ways" is to focus on profit margins and your price points. So ... take a look at what you're selling. What's your best selling product? How quickly can you raise your price on this item (or product line) by AT LEAST 10 per cent?

3) Start getting an idea of what your real numbers are in your business. First, "guesstimate" using the "5 Ways as your guide.

   Then, for the next two weeks, test your conversion rates by ticking off how many people come through your doors (or request information about your business) and who actually buy something. Record the average amount of what they buy. Track to see if they return within that time period.

Now you can start to get a handle on how much you're actually spending to buy your customers, and can start making better decisions based on facts and numbers, instead of guesses and estimates.

Chapter 2:

Allowable Acquisition Costs

To understand Buying Customers, you have to understand acquisition costs and the idea of profit per customer.

There are different ways to define acquisition costs, but for our purposes, let's keep our definitions to two kinds of acquisition costs.

There is Allowable Acquisition Cost, which is the amount a business can spend to bring in a customer the first time they purchase from you.

Understanding Allowable Acquisition Cost and using that number to buy customers gives businesses the possibility of unlimited growth.

If the number is low, businesses can afford to buy as many customers as possible.

There is a second strategy as well, Investment Acquisition Cost.

This is when businesses invest in Buying Customers even though they know they will not make a profit on that customer at the first sale.

Some companies can afford to use an Investment Acquisition strategy because they have the resources to absorb the costs.

For these companies, cashflow isn't a problem.

They can afford a long-term investment because they know they will be around to reap the rewards.

For businesses that don't have that type of cashflow, this kind of strategy can be a trap.

If your strategy is to make profit from customers slowly, over time, but you end up going out of business before you can earn those profits, then it really was the wrong strategy.

This is a problem many businesses face these days.

They get caught between allowable acquisition cost and investment acquisition cost because they don't view their business in terms of profit per customer.

Buying customers isn't about using one strategy or the other.

It's not about allowable acquisition cost strategy being right or investment cost strategy being right, because they both work, depending on the circumstances.

Instead, it's about generating massive profit per customer.

In the end, it's about using the right strategy to bring in as many customers as you want, at a profit.

Luckily, as they say, there are many ways to skin a cat, provided you understand the concept of profit per customer and how it relates to acquisition cost.

You see, the bigger companies that use investment acquisition cost do it because they have the resources and cashflow to wait for their return on investment.

Profit per customer comes a bit further down the road.

In general, smaller businesses need that return as quickly as possible because they can't afford to wait on their profit per customer.

Think about Coca-Cola.

If a bottle of Coke costs about $2, how can they possibly expect to make a profit when they spend so much on advertising?

Well the reason is they expect the customers they buy to remain customers of Coca-Cola for life.

That $2 bottle of Coke isn't the end, it's just the beginning.

Over the lifetime of that customer, they might buy 500 bottles, maybe more and Coca-Cola will see a massive return on investment over time.

For that $1000 per customer spent, Coca-Cola probably earns at least double.

Their profit per customer is outstanding, so they can afford to invest.

For a smaller business, a smaller brand, the investment might be smaller.

The idea is the same, but the cost might be $10 or $100 instead of $1000.

Consider the cost of a networking event that might bring your business more customers.

Hosting an event may cost a couple hundred dollars, so the cost per lead is low.

Many of those attend the event may never become customers, but the ones that do should provide a nice profit over the long term.

Spend a certain amount on a customer and ensure that the customer spends more than that amount buying from you.

That is profit per customer, pure and simple, and the concept is at the heart of whichever acquisition strategy you use.

How Do Successful Businesses Get That Way?

Successful businesses do certain things very well.

They attract new leads, convert those leads to customers and keep those customers coming back, at a profit. In short, they understand the importance of:

1) Lifetime Value

2) Acquisition Costs

3) Conversion Rates

4) Average $ Sale

Once you understand what the drivers of a great business are, it comes down to understanding the goal of your business.

You see, many businesses don't understand what business they are really in, but successful companies understand this concept.

They are in the customer experience business.

Remember, a business is not measured by a trademark, logo, idea or address.

A business simply isn't a business until it has customers who keep coming back.

Once you get leads looking to buy from your business, you must make the most out of every opportunity.

You must turn those prospects into sales and your acquisition cost is, by definition, less than the profit you make on the sale.

So, how many prospects that come through your door are you converting to customers? More importantly, how many prospects walk past your door and never buy from you?

These days every business has a local and virtual address and both can be used to bring potential customers to the business.

How do you use your multiple addresses to drive customers to your business?

Do you know how many people search for your products and services every day?

Investing vs. Spending: How Do You Figure Your Acquisition Cost?

Your acquisition cost is the cost of a given marketing campaign, divided by the number who not only responded, but bought from you.

Imagine you've placed an ad in your local paper that costs $200.

You get 20 responses from your ad and from those, ten actually buy from you.

What is our acquisition cost?

$200/ 10 = $20

For your acquisition cost, you divide the $200 you spent by the 10 customers you got from the ad and it cost you $20 to buy each customer.

Your allowable acquisition cost is just the next step.

Is that $20 too much to spend to buy each customer or is it a price that works for your business?

If your new customer is spending a couple of hundred dollars and leaving more than $20 in profit when they buy from you, that $20 is an allowable acquisition cost, because the cost of buying the customers is covered in the profit.

Basically, if your Allowable Acquisition Cost is more than or equal to that $20 investment, you have a good campaign.

Let's say your business is heavily into internet marketing.

You spend $1000 for pay-per-click ads on a popular search engine.

Your plan is to get 200 people to fill in a form on your site, so your cost is $1000 divided by 200, or $5 per lead.

If only 20 of those 200 people buy, for a 10 percent conversion rate, your cost of customer acquisition is $1000 cost / 20 sales = $50.

If those customers are spending $50 on that first purchase, you're breaking even, so you've got to get them to come back for repeat business to see any profit on that campaign.

What if the average profit is only $10?

You need to rethink that campaign because it's costing you money, unless, of course, you have the resources to handle an Investment

Acquisition Cost strategy and plan on earning your profit on future purchases.

For example, a hairdresser might offer a highlight service to new customers for $30 when it normally costs the customer $100 for the same service.

On the first service, the hairdresser might lose a bit, but they will make it up the next time that customer comes in for highlights, or a cut or even when they buy product.

This strategy won't work if the majority of customers who respond to this offer don't come back, so you must be sure to offer something of great value when using this strategy.

You also have to know exactly what goes into your costs to use it, or any strategy, correctly.

Generally, using an Investment Acquisition Cost strategy is one of the biggest risks a business can take if they don't know their numbers.

But if done correctly the return can make all the difference.

Unfortunately, many businesses use this strategy without even knowing it.

They aren't looking at buying each customer as an investment.

Instead they are viewing the entirety of their marketing as an expense and hoping their campaigns will bring in enough customers, instead of being proactive and knowing what campaigns can work profitably.

You have to know your numbers and test and measure each campaign to ensure your acquisition strategy doesn't end up putting your business behind the eight ball.

Chapter Review – "9 to Grow On"

1) The best businesses focus on 3 key metrics:

   Lifetime value
   Customer Acquisition Costs
   Conversion rates

2) You MUST know your numbers to make good and sound decisions in your business.

3) Knowing your numbers allows you to know what you'll have to pay to continually buy customers at a value price that will generate a return.

4) You have to view your marketing as investing in buying your most important asset, customers.

5) Your allowable acquisition cost is what you can spend to buy a customer at a profit.

6) You can understand the effectiveness of any marketing you do by understanding how effectively you invest in buying your customers.

7) There are two types of customers acquisition strategy, Allowable Acquisition Cost and Investment Acquisition Cost.

8) Allowable Acquisition Cost is best used by businesses that need to stay consistently profitable, week to week and moth to month.

9) Investment Acquisition Cost is best used by companies that have the cashflow to make long-term investments in Buying Customers.

3 Things to DO after your Review:

1) Use your numbers to review your customer acquisition costs, cost per lead and now, cost per sale.

2) Would your company be better served using an Allowable Acquisition Cost Strategy or Investment Cost Strategy?

3) Are there ways to lower your Acquisition Cost by revamping your marketing? What are some ways?

Chapter 3:

Conversion Rates

How Do You Measure Your Marketing?

Often, business know how much their advertising costs and make the mistake of dividing that figure by the number of leads they get rather than the actual number of paying customers.

Sure, it's easier to work out how many people responded to your ad than actually bought, but this creates a problem because you can't truly know how effective an ad is unless you know the actual return you're getting.

You may discover that some forms of marketing bring plenty of inquiries, but a low rate of sales.

Another form of marketing may generate fewer leads but more sales.

This can be confusing for some businesses, but if you aren't sure why some campaigns work and some don't, there's a simple solution: qualify your leads.

Qualify Your Leads

As you test and measure, you may find ads you've previously received good responses from actually generate fewer paying customers than you thought.

This is because you haven't qualified in your ad well enough.

For instance, an ad that says, "Call for you free information kit" will probably attract more callers than an ad that gives an actual call to buy.

Asking people to pay for shipping and handling or a few dollars for a "free kit" also helps to qualify whether someone is just looking or truly interested in buying.

Conversion Rates: What They Are

Conversion rates and customer acquisition costs go hand-in-hand because the better you convert leads into customers, the lower your acquisition cost will be.

Because of this, conversion rate should always be a great focus of your business.

Building a strong conversion rate comes down to great sales ability, value and service.

Through the proper sales training, you can turn each member of your team into a conversion machine because they will know exactly how to show each customer the value of what you sell.

If you show the prospects that come to your business you are outstanding in value and service as well, you will certainly convert them to customers and you will probably even turn them into repeat customers with the end goal of moving them up the loyalty ladder to "Raving Fan".

How many times have you asked yourself how many prospects are you converting to customers?

To find out the percentage you're converting, keep a database of customers and track each and every purchase.

Businesses like department stores and electronics retail stores often ask their customers for their phone numbers during the transaction to help track.

In general, customers are used to being asked for certain information and it allows businesses to know exactly how many customers in their database are actually buying from them.

Measuring Conversion Rates

To measure your conversion rate properly, first pick a starting and ending date on a given marketing campaign.

Then take the number of sales you make during that campaign, divide it by the number of leads and multiply by 100.

That's your conversion rate.

Sales of Period / Number of Leads X 100 = Conversion Rate

A marketing campaign begins on March 1 and will run through the end of the month.

Over that time, the business finds the campaign has produced 5000 inquiries or phone calls.

Over that time 1250 sales were made, leading to a conversion rate of 25 percent.

1250 / 5000 X 100 = 25 percent

No business should ever assume a person's natural interest in their products will make them a customer and without measuring a business can't pinpoint the issues that are plaguing it.

Conversion rate is so poorly understood and thought of that when I ask people in business what their conversion rates are, they usually aren't sure, so they take a guess.

That's simply not good enough.

You have to measure it.

Let's say a business hands out flyers to people walking on their street.

The campaign generates 1000 leads over a 2 week period, but just 100 of those leads buy.

1000 leads / 100 new customers = 10 percent conversion rate

The conversion rate is just 10 percent, but now the business can begin to figure out where they are going wrong.

Maybe their customer service is poor.

Maybe the target of their campaign was wrong, maybe the offer they made wasn't good enough.

Whatever the limiting factors, knowing is half the battle to overcoming them.

Now say that same business tries a different campaign, placing an ad in their local newspaper for two weeks.

Over that time they generate just 600 leads, but 200 of those leads buy from them.

600 leads / 200 new customers = 33.3 percent conversion rate

Why is the second campaign so much more successful?

What factors may contribute to the difference?

With just the information given, a business can begin to figure out what works for them.

Overestimation Can Lead to Trouble

There was a business owner I worked with years ago, who could never seem to get enough customers.

I remember when I asked her about her conversion rate, she guessed that she sold to "80 or 85 percent" of the people who called or came through her doors.

We did some serious testing and measuring and found that the number was closer to 35 percent.

It came as a big shock to her, but it also signaled an outstanding opportunity because she was missing out on loads of new customers.

Once we worked on some methods of converting prospects to customers, her business practically took off.

Think of the difference in the bottom line that comes from significantly boosting your conversion rate.

If you can take your conversion rate from 30 to 60 percent, you've doubled your revenue.

Growing your conversion rate comes down to one question.

What is your business?

Are you in the business of producing what you sell or are you in the customer experience business, the business of Buying Customers who will use your services over and over again?

As we discussed earlier, every business is in the customer experience business.

If you have a business that produces products rather than meets the needs of potential customers, this is a very important idea to consider when approaching the challenges you surely face.

Your business is about generating profits and you get there Buying Customers, not focusing exclusively on producing what you sell.

> Almost all quality improvement comes via simplification of design, manufacturing... layout, processes, and procedures.
>
> *Tom Peters*

Sell What People Want to Buy: Customer Experience

Most businesses are proud of the products their company produces and those products become the focus of everything in and around the business.

For these owners, it's important to remember that you can never be better, faster or cheaper than your competition all the time.

Sure, you have to have a quality product that people want, but there will always be someone who offers what you offer in terms of products or pricing.

So if you can't separate yourself from your competition through your products or pricing, you differentiate yourself from the competition by focusing on customer service, which leads to earning and keeping customers for a long time, the end goal of Buying Customers.

Nordstrom Sets a High Standard in Customer Service

Few businesses have the commitment to customer service that retailer Nordstrom has.

Nordstrom thrives on providing legendary experiences through unbelievable customer service, which result in customer folklore and the most powerful word-of-mouth possible.

Legends of Nordstrom's pampering of customers are widespread.

Every register at Nordstrom stores has pen and paper for customers to share their stories.

Every morning before each store opens, Nordstrom employees gather in the main lobby for the store manager to share some of the best stories from the previous day and reward the employees in those stories.

To ensure great customer service, each new employee receives a handbook with the following right up front: "We're glad to have you with our Company.

Our number one goal is to provide outstanding customer service. Set both your personal and professional goals high.

We have great confidence in your ability to achieve them."

An Evolving Investment

Say you spent $1000 on an advertisement.

How many customers would have to buy from you to make that ad break even?

From that $1000, what is your cost per lead?

What is your cost per sale?

What is Your Cost per Lead?

Generating leads is often one of the most expensive areas of a business, so keeping cost per lead within the range of your Allowable Acquisition Cost is very important.

The most cost effective way to generate leads is through referrals but today, with the importance of targeted marketing, everything a small business does needs to be predicated on cost per lead reasonably low and profitable for the business in general.

If a marketing campaign costs a business $4000 and it generates 50 leads, that business is spending $80 per lead.

$4000/50 Leads = $80/lead

What is Your Cost per Sale?

Following that same example, if, of those 50 leads, 20 sales were made, the cost of that campaign per sale is $200.

$4000/20 Sales = $200/sale

But to get to the heart of the matter, you have to dig a bit deeper.

There are so many factors that go into your cost per sale, including your overhead costs, cost per lead and how much you spend to buy your customers.

To truly understand this number, you have to spell out each resource you expend in your business then divide that number by each sale you make.

This is incredibly important because this is how you figure out when you break even and begin to run in profits in your business.

You can use this number to figure out your break even and profit per day, week, month and even year.

Wouldn't it be great to know what time of the day you break even?

That way you could plan and exploit trends in your customer base for the most possible gain for your business.

Your cost per sale can be determined by different factors.

Your customers aren't the only thing you buy in a business.

In fact, as you well know, you pay for everything in your business, including each sale you make.

Start by figuring out what the average amount a customer spends the first time they buy from you.

Do they spend $50, $100, $200 on an average sale?

Let's say that $1000 investment generates 200 leads and 50 of those leads buy, spending a total of $4000.

$1000/200 leads = $5 per lead

$1000/50 sales = $20 per sale

Once you have those numbers, you can decide just how much you are willing to spend to buy each and every customer that comes into your business.

From these numbers, we also know the campaign itself was profitable.

But what about the other costs in your business?

Let's say you own an auto repair shop.

You've started a new loyalty campaign with the hopes it will bring you new customers through referrals from your best customers.

To get the campaign moving, you decide to invest $2000 in special events and items that you will reward your customers with for their continued business with you.

You decide to throw a seminar where your distributors will talk about how to use their products correctly, while giving your attendees some great extra information about maintaining their cars.

Next, you decide to offer those same customers a free oil change when they refer their friends to you.

During the first three months of this campaign, you have gained over 100 new leads and 50 new customers.

The average amount each of those new customers spent with you on each sale was $50.

Some just got oil changes, some got their brakes done, but on average they spent $50.

Now let's go through the numbers.

Cost per Lead: $2000/100 leads = $20

Cost per Sale: $2000/50 sales = $40

So it cost our repair shop $20 to bring in those leads and $40 to buy an actual customer.

Since we know that each customer spends on average, $50, we know that the shop profits $10 on each new customer.

Still, that doesn't consider all of the shop's costs-which shows why it is so important to know all of your numbers and how they factor into any new campaign.

However, knowing that the average person spends $50 and you make $10 gives you something most don't have, the power to control and adjust your pricing upward.

By adding value, our auto shop now has the ability to manage not only costs, but profits by knowing what numbers it needs to focus on.

Oncosts, On-Going Cost and Overhead

Your business is a profit making machine.

That is what your business should be producing every day.

When you have this focus on your business, it is far easier to understand that everything that happens in your business is related.

At the same time, each part of your profit making machine has a cost, an investment you've made in it.

All of these expenses need to be considered and factored when you undertake a new marketing campaign.

One way to look at this is like, "The Butterfly Effect."

A butterfly would flap its wings in Australia and it would cause a tornado in Kansas.

In some ways business is just like that.

The slightest thing can have a big effect if you aren't careful.

That's why you have to be sure to factor everything into your plans.

The price of Buying Customers should be reflected in every cost in your business, including your oncosts, or company overhead.

I've never felt like I was in the cookie business. I've always been in a feel good feeling business. My job is to sell joy. My job is to sell happiness. My job is to sell an experience.

Debbi Fields

Knowing All of Your Numbers

You may be spending $1600 per month in marketing, but if that $1600 doesn't bring in enough leads, and you don't convert enough of those leads to customers, or if those customers aren't spending enough each time they buy from you, it may affect other parts of your business.

After all, that $1600 per month in marketing isn't the only expense in your business.

You have to pay for the building, your team, your products, everything that goes into running your business every day.

Without factoring in your weekly or monthly costs into your marketing, you are losing part of the equation.

For a restaurant in that situation, the quality of the food might drop because the owner wouldn't be able to afford high quality anymore.

That drop in quality might lead to a drop in customers.

The business might slow down and now the restaurant can only spend $1000 a month on marketing or they can take the money from other areas of their profit making machine.

The "Five Ways" are incredibly important because they serve to help your oncosts in every aspect of a business while helping businesses focus on creating lifetime value, customer acquisition cost and conversion rates and average dollar sale for their profit making machine.

These on-going costs can also be factored into your cost per lead and cost per sale to get a completely accurate reading of how much money you are investing in your business over a given time.

Franchisees Don't Have it Their Way

One of the benefits of working in a franchise system is nothing is left to chance.

Systems are spelled out and the local franchises follow those systems to profit.

But that hasn't been the case for many operators of a burger franchise who have been losing money thanks to the company's value menu.

It seems that a double cheeseburger that customers buy for a dollar costs each individual restaurant more than a dollar to make.

Because of the item's popularity this situation has caused some hardships among franchisees.

This is a great example of how existing costs in a business can have a dramatic effect on the bottom line.

Sure, the burger franchise wants to bring as many customers as possible through the door but a dollar double cheeseburger proved costly as a loss leader.

Rather than bringing in repeat customers, each customer that only buys this item once from the value menu becomes a drain on the resources of the individual restaurant, and no business stays healthy by losing money when customers buy just one time from them.

> Sometimes when you innovate, you make mistakes. It is best to admit them quickly, and get on with improving your other innovations.
>
> *Steve Jobs*

The Baker

I once knew a baker who spent $300 a week on advertising, week after week.

When I asked him how many new customers his advertising brought in every week, he said he had no idea.

Even when he estimated, his advertising's effectiveness was positively worthless.

He guessed that the $300 he spent every week brought in 10 new customers.

Now this wasn't some high end boutique, this was a neighborhood bakery and the average amount each customer bought from him was only $4.50.

By his own estimation he was losing $25.50 per customer per week in his marketing, yet he still bought those ads, week after week.

He was not happy to learn how he had been throwing money away, but at the same time he was happy to learn that his business had massive room for improvement and it wouldn't take too much to find a more effective way of marketing than the one he was using.

Do you know what the scariest part of this story is?

The fact that so many businesses do just what the baker did.

He was not alone back then, and today, more than 20 years later, I know this practice still hasn't stopped.

There are still businesses all over the world throwing money away on advertising because they don't understand the concept of customer acquisition cost and, to a deeper extent, don't really understand what kind of business they are truly in.

So what did I do to help the baker?

First I had to get his acquisition cost down.

In fact, I wanted to get it under a dollar, since he was selling inexpensive, yet potentially high volume, baked goods.

How could he add value to his offer?

To me, one delicious yet inexpensive item on the menu was his chocolate éclair.

This was decades ago and it's safe to say I probably ate way too many of those while working with him.

Anyway, I asked him how much it cost to make the éclairs.

He said it cost him about thirty cents per éclair, and I knew we were on our way to our goal.

Armed with a plan, I told him it was time to change his marketing strategy, but we actually just had to change his advertising, so we printed loads of flyers offering a free éclair to new customers.

His response was classic and is one of the main reasons this story sticks with me to this day.

"Do you realize how many people will come in for a free éclair? How will we deal with all of those new customers?" he asked me.

I reminded him of what a good problem that is to have because getting all of those new customers was obviously the point of advertising.

Not only was the new campaign an improvement, we were blown away by the response to the new offer.

Let's run the numbers:

Our printed advert cost $300 and if it brought in 300 customers, our acquisition cost was just $1 on the advertisement, but that wasn't the only factor to consider.

There was also the cost of the éclair.

The baker spent just thirty cents to make each éclair, so we were able to buy each customer for just $1.30.

While this already seems like a success story, it turned out the ad was even more successful then we imagined.

Sixteen out of 17 new customers bought other things while they were at the bakery, spending about $4.50 the first time.

So for the investment of just $1.30 per customer, the baker earned $4.50 on the first purchase, then with some sales training we were able to boost that average dollar sale to $5.50.

Do you think he was happy with that strategy?

We estimated that the new flyer would bring in about 300 people in the first week, but in reality it brought in closer to 600.

It was a crush of customers for a sleepy little bakery, but it proved the power of how to market correctly.

No longer was the baker just spending good money after bad with no real concept of his return on investment.

He had set real goals and achieved them by targeting his advertising with a focus on what he did best, his chocolate éclair.

The bakery had more customers than it could handle for a short time, until we trained the team at the bakery to deal with customers efficiently through scripts and other customer service training.

This training meant that the new customers didn't just show for a one time offer, they came back time and again.

They weren't just converted into customers.

They were converted to raving fans of the baker's business.

Branding or Leads? What's More Important?

What is more important to a business ... building a brand or getting more leads?

Many creative types who work in ad agencies and love to spend other's money, would immediately respond "branding."

After all, without a brand, how do you drive customers to your business?

But think of it another way.

Without leads, how do you build a brand?

In the world of truly building a business through systemized marketing, getting new customers isn't about "creative" or high concept layouts.

Remember our formula, "Target, Offer, Copy."

When you start to look at marketing this way, it simply becomes a matter of math.

If your ads generate cost effective leads for your business, you've got a good ad.

If it doesn't, you don't.

This is a hard lesson for a lot of people to deal with.

But if you start to adopt a truly marketing-driven business mindset, you'll soon realize you care less about being creative and more about the tactics and strategies that will drive leads into your company ... at a profit.

That's the only way to turn your marketing "expenses" into "investments" and the only way to start buying customers that give you a great ROI over time.

After all, how many of us could afford to continually buy a share of stock for $10 and sell it for $5?

That said, why would we continue to buy an ad or run a marketing campaign that doesn't make us money?

So ... when it comes to "Branding or Leads" ... it's less a "Chicken and Egg" conversation and more of an "Expense or Investment" conversation.

In the end ... if you get enough leads and enough business, you'll build the best kind of brand there is: a company that is loved for your customers' reasons rather than your own.

Say you're starting a new business and you work out that you will need 1000 customers in total for your new business to be profitable.

If it costs your new business $100 to buy a customer, then you need a marketing budget of $100,000 to effectively buy customers and generate a profit.

Most new companies never do this math and wonder why they don't ever get profitable.

What if you don't have $100,000, but you can only spend $50,000 to generate new customers.

What can you do?

Maybe you have to get the other $50,000 over time from sales.

Or, you'll have to be prepared to run at a loss for maybe the entirety of year one, while ensuring you have a good system for repeat business in place and position yourself for profit in year two.

Knowing your numbers gives you tremendous leverage and an advantage in your decision making for your business in terms of how you spend your resources, while also giving you the power to adjust your strategy based on your market.

Chapter Review – "9 to Grow On"

1) Your conversion rate is the number of sales you get from the number of leads that come into your business.

2) Total number of Sales in a Period / Total Number of Leads = Conversion Rate
Multiply this by 100 to get your answer in percentage terms.

   An example:
   1250 sales / 5000 leads = .25
   .25 X 100 = 25 per cent

3) Your cost per sale is simply what you are spending to buy a sale.

4) For example … a $1000 ad generates 200 leads and 50 sales.
$1000 ad / 200 leads = $5 per lead (cost per lead)
$1000 / 50 sales = $20 per sale (cost per sale)

5) Your cost per sale will allow you to effectively determine how much you are willing to spend to buy each and every customer that comes into your business.

6) Even big companies can get into trouble when they don't know all of their numbers. Burger King and its double cheeseburger promotion is a great example.

7) Once you know your numbers, you can start making better decisions that both control costs and grow your sales and bottom-line.

8) Added value and existing resources that can be turned into offers more than likely already exist in your business.

9) Coming up with easy ways to leverage these resources can have a dramatic impact on your company. The case study of the baker and the éclair is just one example.

3 Things to DO after your Review:

1) Can you go after a better target, devise a better offer, use better copy? Can you up the price of a first purchase, or create a bundle of items to add value?

2) Think of some campaigns or programs you may have run that you could revive or re-purpose with you new found numbers knowledge. What types of added value can you bundle? How could you lower your costs and up your sales?

3) What specific products or services do you already have in stock, inventory or that you sell that could easily be turned into an offer to drive more leads and traffic to your business? What type of older inventory or slower moving products could be used for the same?

Chapter 4:

What is Lifetime Value?

Once you know what you can spend on acquisition cost and you begin generating new customers, you have to know how to keep them coming back.

This is where the ideas behind Investment Acquisition Cost take hold, because they are predicated on the lifetime value of the customer.

But no matter what strategy you use, repeat business equals a strong business.

Let's start our discussion of lifetime value with some simple numbers.

If your average customer spends $20 every time they buy and they buy from you 3 times per year and you can expect to have the customer for 5 years, what is that customer's lifetime value to your business?

Let's do the math.

$20 X 3 = $60

$60 X 5 years = $300

Each customer has an average lifetime value of $300.

This is a simple equation but one that raises the question that is the crux of this book, "How much are you willing to pay to buy a customer?"

One type of business that uses the lifetime value scenario really well is gyms.

Often gyms give away free enrollment because they know they will recoup that fee over the lifetime of their customers, in monthly fees.

Let's say the average lifespan of a gym member is three years and they spend $20 a month on their membership.

$20 X 12 months X 3 years.

= $240 X 3 = $720

$240 is the yearly value of the customer $720 is their lifetime value.

Not a bad deal – for the gym, especially if they can increase the volume of memberships.

The numbers are different in every business … and it's important you know the numbers in yours.

The Expanding Benefits of Lifetime Value

To calculate the lifetime value of a customer you really need to work out how much one customer will spend with you over the course of 12 months and then what they would spend over three, five years or the number of years they have a buying relationship with you.

The other factor is how many friends that customer will refer to a business over the course of those years.

Your first ads may run at a loss but if that customer keeps coming back regularly and refers friends to you, you've bought a profitable customer.

Let's say you spent $20 per lead and you generated 100 leads, so your campaign cost about $2000.

Of those 100 leads, 40 of them became customers, spending an average of $50 each of the two times they bought from you in the first year.

The average lifetime of a customer is 2 years.

From those numbers we can figure out the lifetime value of each of these customers is $200.

With 40 new customers and a lifetime value of $200, the campaign generated about $8000.

40 new customers X $200 lifetime value= $8000

40 customers is just the tip of the iceberg.

Say some of those customers are happy with the service they received and tell their friends.

If 10 customers tell one friend who buys from you, all of a sudden that campaign has generated $10,000.

40 new customers + 10 referrals X $200 lifetime value = $10,000

Keep all of this in mind with your marketing.

It's not just the people who come from the first ad but how much profit you're going to make from them and their referrals over the course of several years.

Remember it's all about wallet share, not market share.

A lot of business owners go out looking for market share.

They look to get the largest slice of a potential market for their product or service.

I prefer to look at wallet share, or the amount of money I make from each customer who responds to my ad, over a period of time.

When you take focus away from market share and start looking at wallet share and how it relates to the concept of lifetime value, that's when you start to make real profits from your marketing.

The most important step is turning those new customers you've just bought into lifetime customers.

So how do you create lifetime customers?

Outstanding customer service and added value are the main reasons your customers will return to you.

Through great customer service, businesses add perceived value to the experience of shopping with them.

No matter what they buy, customers want great service.

When you start there and build relationships on that foundation, you will find that generating repeat business is easier than you thought it could be.

Repeat Business = Profits

I believe strong businesses run on one basic principle: repeat business equals profits.

If it costs a business $200 to acquire a customer but that customer only spends $100 when they buy, when does that business show profit?

Obviously the second visit is the break even on cashflow and each visit after that is where you start to make profit.

Without repeat business, any business is destined to fail because many businesses actually lose money on the first sale or two to any customer.

It is only through repeat business that businesses can generate real cash flow and profits.

Once you've made a sale, you need to make another and another and another to the same person because, more often than not, it costs six or seven times more to get a new customer than it does selling to an old one.

Of course, the time frame you use to determine lifetime value is different for each type of business.

If you sell cars, your average customer might buy only once or twice every few years, but they may buy other lower cost products.

A car dealership earns repeat business through add on services.

If a person buys a new car on average every five years, the dealership has to use maintenance to build relationships and keep their repeat business strong.

For a fast food restaurant, the process would be different because there isn't one big purchase at the beginning and items are bought much more frequently.

The average amount bought each time is low, but the frequency with which a customer buys is at a much higher rate.

Retail stores might use a completely different model where small purchases are the beginning of the relationship which leads to bigger purchases.

No matter which of these scenarios your business falls into, the people that do business with you represent a gold mine of opportunity.

You must collect their details, get to know them, treat them well, keep in contact and regularly invite them back.

These people are either going to make you rich or poor.

Businesses have to focus on finding customers who will be with them for the long term.

And then find ways to make them advocates and ravings fans, because then, your customers will tell others about how great your business is.

So, what is the overall approach you take with your business?

Do you just sell products or are you offering your ideal customers extra value to move them up the loyalty ladder and ensure they become raving fans of your business?

Do you educate them about your business, the services you offer and everything you sell?

Do they feel special when they buy from you?

Teach Your Customers to be Great

Every time you educate your customers about how to go about doing business with you, you are creating an advocate for life, as long as you fill one condition: always give them the service you've promised them.

It doesn't even have to be Five-Star service so long as it's the service you promised.

But no matter what level of service you've promised, it has to be first rate.

Another tip: be sure to let high quality customers know you're looking for more customers just like them.

You'll be giving them a huge compliment and setting a standard for who they will refer to you right away.

The Raving Fan

The ultimate goal is to create an advocate for life, or what I call, "raving fans" of your business.

Raving fans don't just happen. Businesses have to work hard to get customers to that point.

There are seven types of people every business deals with, the suspect, the prospect, the shopper, the customer, the member, the advocate and, finally, the raving fan.

When people first start out on the loyalty ladder, at the bottom rung, they are suspects.

They are only potential customers at this stage.

They fit within your target market and are willing to buy from you if it's convenient.

The next step up, these prospects are now suspects who have taken some sort of action.

They may have called in response to an ad or shown some sort of interest in your business.

This is the stage it's most important to get their contact information so you can stay in touch.

Customer loyalty is about relationship building and any business' goal is to build a database of prospects and move them up to the next stage as shoppers.

Prospects become shoppers when they have bought from you once.

This level is that many businesses put that huge stop sign up, even though they may not realize they are doing it.

The stop sign is simply waiting for these customers to return rather than actively inviting them back.

You have to remember that at this level your customers are probably costing you money to buy, not making it, so getting them to come back is vital.

If you actively invite all of your shoppers back, imagine the possibilities for your business.

That stop sign is the scariest thing I've come across in business.

You need to get rid of it, and fast, if you want your business to grow and your customers to move up the ladder.

To be classified as a customer, the next step on the ladder, your shopper needs to have spent money or done business with you and you need to have recorded the sale in your records.

You need to record this in your records because it allows you to differentiate between prospects and customers in your database.

Why should you do this?

If you are planning to send out a letter to all prospects offering them an incentive to buy, you don't want to send that same letter to people that are already shoppers or customers.

Keeping track of these records will also tell you when they last bought, how often they buy and what their average dollar sale is, all incredibly important.

When your customers feel like they belong, they become members.

This is really the most important threshold to reach with your customers because those that make two purchases are ten times more likely to keep buying from you than those customers that only make one purchase.

That's why you need to put some effort into your members.

You can give them a membership card or membership pack and in that pack you can include a brochure of every product and service you offer.

Include samples, vouchers and other things that will drive customers to return to you.

Next up is the advocate.

These are customers who sell you to other people.

They give referrals, promote you and keep on buying.

This group of customers is one of your major assets because they are like another group of sales people, and they help to keep customer acquisition costs low.

Finally there is the raving fan, the level you would like all of your customers to achieve.

There is a simple, yet important difference between an advocate and a raving fan.

While an advocate will sell for you, a raving fan can't help but promote you.

They talk about your business all the time and they can almost be regarded as part of your team because they cultivate so much business for you.

The reason raving fans are so important for your business is very simple.

Repeat business equals a successful business.

Happy Customer to Raving Fan

Some businesses pay very little attention to keeping a close relationship with their existing customers.

Those businesses would have little idea who their existing customers are and how to make contact with them.

Think about most of the restaurants in your town.

Have you ever received a letter from any of your favorites asking you to dine with them again?

Did they even get your contact details?

Probably not, but you can be sure that there is advertising all over town in an effort to gain new customers.

Does this make sense when it comes to Buying Customers?

Of course it doesn't.

How much easier and cheaper would it be to focus marketing

efforts on the customers that restaurant already has?

Another benefit is that focusing on existing customers allows businesses to predict future requirements and cashflow.

They've already started buying, so they aren't a mystery and you've already invested the money in the first place, so why not make them happy?

Happy customers are always willing to return because they feel comfortable with that business.

People like to avoid the unknown and don't like taking chances when it comes to what they buy, so cultivating existing customers to return time and again is far easier if they are comfortable and happy with your business.

These customers will pay dividends for your business for years, and if you're lucky enough, for decades.

> Profit in business comes from repeat customers, customers that boast about your project or service, and that bring friends with them.
>
> *W. Edwards Deming*

The Empire Strikes Back

Do you have any friends that are fans of the "Star Wars" movies? The original, now referred to as "The New Hope" was released in the late 1970's and its aftermath remains one of the great marketing success stories ever told.

Think about all of those kids that bought Star Wars action figures and other toys when the original movies came out. Now fast forward to today. How much money do you think each of those kids has spent on Star Wars as they became adults?

Odds are they've spent quite a bit. Through books, graphic novels, clothing, television shows, DVDs and other assorted items, the creators of Star Wars have made millions, if not billions of dollars over the years. And they didn't do it by making just movies. They created an entire culture and with that culture they built a huge database of lifetime customers.

The original movie, made in 1977, cost about $11 million American to make. Now think about how many hundreds of millions have been made by the franchise.

Most small businesses aren't going to be able generate the kind of buzz that Star Wars has for nearly 40 years, but through this story you can see just how important the lifetime value of a customer is.

By many estimations, since the release of the first movie, most people who consider themselves Star Wars fans have spent anywhere from $1000 to $3000 on memorabilia, and those estimates seem conservative.

These fans spend the money because they have a deep affinity for the series and they identify with the culture of Star Wars. Do you make your customers feel the same way?

Your Customers: A, B, C and D

There are four categories of customers and prospects and I list them as A, B, C and D customers.

So why grade your customers?

Like everything in any business, you've got to test and measure to see what avenues are most and least cost effective.

It's the same for customers.

Each customer is not equal.

Some are a pleasure to deal with and don't cost you extra time and money, while others are a drag on every aspect of your business.

Who would you rather do business with, a customer who is pleasant, doesn't fight you and makes the buying process easy or someone who is argumentative, nasty and always finds a reason they shouldn't pay full price?

The choice is easy isn't it?

Unfortunately, many businesses spend their time trying to make their worst customers happy rather than focusing on making their best customers even happier and building that relationship.

When you really think about it, why waste time trying to make someone happy who is perpetually looking for the negative?

Grading customers is another, effective tool to use in determining how to buy customers because you can determine just how good your service is.

If you grade your customers and find that a very small percentage are "A" customers, while most are "C" and "D" customers, you can begin to understand why you aren't getting as many referrals as you'd like and find a way to overcome the challenge.

By grading your customers, you can determine where your efforts will be best served to develop the return on investment you need from your customers.

Finally, by grading your customers, you will be to provide the best possible service with the best possible return for your business because you know which of your customers are worth investing in.

So, while we split our customers into four groups, what do those groupings mean?

Here's an easy way to remember exactly what they stand for.

A Customers are Awesome.

B Customers are Basic.

C Customers are ones you Can't deal with.

D Customers are to be considered Dead to your business.

So what do these customers typically look like, how would you recognize them if they came into your business?

Grade A customers will usually spend more money and be less of a hassle than the rest.

This group is the key to generating multitudes of referrals.

Grade B customers are good, solid customers who may well be the backbone of the average small business.

This group is more price conscious but not to the point of being difficult or a nuisance.

Grade C customers demand a lot of your time, haggle on price and take forever to make up their mind.

Grade D customers are every business owner's nightmare.

They pay their bills late, make frequent returns and just take up loads of your time for little return.

This group has even been known to make scenes in stores if they don't get their way.

They simply aren't worth having as customers.

Of course you only want to deal with the A's and B's if at all possible.

If that's the case, there are two things you can do.

You can move your "C" and "D" customer up or you can simply get rid of them.

If you want to get rid of them, you can just explain to them the cost of doing business has simply become too much for your business.

You might even be able to sell them off to one of your competitors by explain that "XYZ company" will be servicing them from now on.

With this strategy, everyone can be happy.

You can make a few dollars selling that list of difficult customers to a competitor, the competitor will think they've gotten a bargain with all their new customers and the customers will still have someone to take care of their needs.

Only you will know that group of customers is more trouble than they are worth.

There are many ways to move your worst customers either up the loyalty ladder or out the door.

You should setup rules your customers have to follow in order to do business with your company.

Then write to everyone in your database explaining that you are repositioning your company and these are the new rules.

You can change your pricing policy to weed out the C's and D's or even change your business' décor.

For example, I remember hearing about a video store that wanted to get rid of a young group of toughs who gathered there.

The video store simply changed the music they played from pop to classical and their client base changed virtually overnight.

Just 20 percent of your customers account for about 80 percent of your business.

Do you know who your 20 percent is?

These are the customers you should be concentrating on.

Remember it only takes one bad customer to ruin your entire day, but loads of them can ruin your business.

You can either ruin or make the day of your other customers by how you feel when you serve them, so take the time to decide which qualities you want your new customers to have before you put strategies in place to attract them.

At this point you need to do some self-analysis.

It's time to write your own criteria for a grade "A" customer.

Sit down and imagine your ideal customer.

- How often do they buy from you, what do they buy, when do they buy it?

- What is the underlying desire they are filling when they buy from you?

- What do you have to do to ensure they will buy from you again?

- Ask yourself whether your new customers would want to do business with you.

Or look at it from another point of view.

- What do you need to change to have them want to do business with you?

Now, as I mentioned, it's not strictly about moving your worst customers out, it's also about moving them up as best you can.

You can start by sending a letter detailing your new way of doing business to your C and D customers.

Some will abide by the new rules and may even become B or even A customers while others will want to go elsewhere.

Either way, once you've moved all of your C and D customers up or out, the next step is to train your B customers to become A customers.

Again you can do this with a simple letter detailing all the great benefits derived from being a top customer with your business.

Let your A customers know you can now devote far more time to their needs, more time and energy on outstanding service and, of course, ask them for referrals.

Remember that if you give great service to your D customers they'll generally refer more D customers to you and you want referrals from your A customers, not your D customers.

The people you love to do business with, the ones who meet your criteria for being A customers are the ones you should be chasing.

By the time you've completed this exercise every client will be aware of the type of customer you want to deal with, but you must make it clear you are doing this so you can provide the best possible service to your customers.

This is how you'll generate the repeat customers who equate to profits and a thriving business.

Chapter Review – "9 to Grow On"

1) Lifetime Value is one of the most important, yet most overlooked and least understood metric in business. But it's also one of the simplest to understand.

2) Lifetime Value is simply the amount of revenue/turnover you can expect from your typical customer, based on the Average Value/Amount they buy X the number of times they buy from you X the average length of time they are a customer.

3) In a simple example, your average customer spends $20 every time they buy from you; they buy from you 3 times per year, and you can expect to have the customer for 5 years, the Lifetime Value of that customer is $300.

   For example:
   $20 average spend X 3 transactions = $60 revenue/turnover
   $60 revenue/turnover X 5 years = $300

4) Once you understand Lifetime Value, you can start to see the power of repeat business and its affect on profit. You can also start to see the importance of referrals as fueling your repeat business.

5) Most companies don't PROFIT on repeat business until the fifth or even sixth transaction.

6) One way to profit more quickly is to lower your cost of buying customers while upping the price points of what they initially or sequentially buy from you.

7) Different businesses use different models for generating repeat business. What works for a car dealership won't necessarily work for a fast food restaurant.

8) Determining your Cost Per Lead will help you make better decisions on how you spend dollars to buy those leads.

9) Cost Per Lead = Cost of your Ad/Total Number of Leads Generated

   For example:

   If a marketing campaign costs you $4000 and generates 50 leads, you're spending $80 per lead.

   $4000 / 50 Leads= $80 per lead

3 Things to DO after your Review:

1) Sit down and first "guesstimate" what your acquisition cost and the cost per lead for your business is. Then do the numbers to see what it really is. How can you lower those numbers by focusing on the lifetime value of your customers?

2) What can you do to move your customers up the loyalty ladder? Can you think of 5 strategies?

3) How can you keep your Raving Fans happy with your service and telling their friends about your business? Think of 5 strategies.

Chapter 5:
The Principles of Lifetime Value

As we've already discussed, without cultivating the Lifetime Value of your best customers, your business will probably struggle.

This chapter contains some principles that make it easier to understand why Lifetime Value is so important which will help us understand how to use the strategies to create lifetime value in the next chapter.

The 9 Basic Needs of the Customer

According to the school of "Human Scale Development" there are nine basic human needs.

Understanding these needs can help businesses figure out just why people buy from them.

1) Subsistence: This simply means being physically and mentally healthy. People need food, shelter and work to live. Does your business speak to these needs?

2) Protection: Protection is felt through care, adaptability or autonomy. Security and systems play a part here. Guarantees help people feel protected when they buy.

3) Affection: The qualities of affection tend to be respect, sense of humor or even generosity. Friendships, family and quality relationships highlight this quality.

4) Understanding: Understanding means using one's critical capacity, curiosity and even intuition to investigate or analyze. People will turn to literature, experts or education to understand things.

5) Participation: To lead a productive, happy life, people need to have both responsibilities and rights. Dedication and a sense of humor are two qualities that accompany participation.

6) Leisure: Leisure inspires imagination, tranquility and spontaneity in people. Generally, people turn to games, or they may go to parties or just use down time to create leisure.

7) Creation: People need to use their abilities and skills to feel creative. Imagination, boldness, inventiveness and curiosity are qualities of this.

8) Identity: Often people use what they buy to create or build their identity, but language, religion and values are other aspects. A sense of belonging, self-esteem and consistency grow from identity.

9) Freedom: Autonomy and open-mindedness are two major parts of what makes freedom so important to people. In general, people want to feel equal to others and free to make decisions.

Take a look at the list and start to think of each in terms of your own business.

Which of these nine basic human needs is your business speaking to?

Which could it speak to?

How often?

Once you've targeted some basic needs that match and mirror what you offer in your business, you can consider some strategies to communicate how you can meet those needs with you own products, services, helpful insight and information that you can make unique and exclusive to you.

> Above all, we wish to avoid having a dissatisfied customer. We consider our customers a part of our organization and we want them to feel free to make any criticism they see fit in regard to our merchandise or service. Sell practical, tested merchandise at reasonable profit, treat your customers like human beings-and they will always come back.
>
> *L.L Bean*

The Pareto Principle

The 80/20 rule or the Pareto Principle means that 80% of your business usually comes from 20% of your customers.

Of course, those aren't hard and fast numbers.

For your business, the ratio might be 70/30, (or even 60/40) but the principle is the same.

It's up to you to figure out the exact numbers for your business, but it basically works like this:

As we have discussed, there are four types of customers, A, B, C and D.

Knowing this is the case, you need to do two things with your customer base.

You need to lavish your top 20% of customers with attention and great service, while spending less time chasing the bottom 20% who create 80% of the complaints about your business.

For example, when I was still coaching individual businesses, I worked with an insurance company.

They weren't doing as well as they would've liked but they had a lot of customers.

I asked them to draw up a list of their customers, from best to worst and then I drew a line separating the top customers from the bottom 80%.

I told them to "sell" those customers, and at first, the management of that insurance company thought I was crazy.

They thought they couldn't just give up customers.

Finally, I convinced them to sell those customers to their competition and focus on that top 20%.

Guess what happened?

They had their most profitable year ever.

Why?

Because they were able to offer more to the good customers they had while massively reducing overheads.

Profits from add on services grew exponentially and they had more time to devote to customer service and keeping their happy customers happy.

Remember, there are people out there who appreciate good service and are willing to pay for it and there are people who enjoy creating misery for others.

The key to using the 80/20 rule is to understand which is which for your business and cater to those who appreciate your value.

Imagine how loyal your "20%" customers would be if you spent 80% of your time looking after their needs.

Instead, business owners often get it backwards.

They spend too much time trying to make the perpetually unhappy customers happy and get complacent with the satisfied ones.

That is a sure way to build a struggling business.

Focus on your best 20% and your business is sure to see rewards.

So how do you differentiate between the different segments of customers you have?

More importantly, how do you turn your "C" and "D" customers around while gaining more outstanding ones?

By educating them on what is expected of them and holding them to it.

This works, as long as you hold up your end of the bargain.

Actual vs. Current Customers

To truly take advantage of all the opportunities that Lifetime Value can bring your business, it's important to remember that there may be a gap between your current group of customers and your actual database of customers.

Basically, you might have a group of customers that buy from you right now.

You recognize them, you know their needs and work hard to fill those needs.

But for most businesses, that group is just the tip of the iceberg.

To really grow your cashflow and build a profitable business, you have to find ways to reach your actual customer base, or everyone who has bought from you, not just your current customers.

So how do you go about doing that?

Staying in contact with all of your customers is a great way to avoid that pitfall.

In my business, we send postcards, letters, newsletters and offers to all of our clients every month as a way to keep in touch and stay on top of their awareness.

If those customers have coaching needs, even if they haven't worked with my company in years, they are still more likely to come to us to fill those needs because we are still the first thing they think of when it comes to business coaching.

The postcards, newsletters and other publications that we issue to our actual customers, not just our current ones, are the reason for that.

Don't Be Afraid to Ask

Of course, your ultimate goal is to turn those customers into raving fans so they will bring you tons of referrals.

Referrals don't happen by accident.

Your customer service should be good enough to bring customers back and get them to tell their friends, but a lot of the time that still isn't enough to build referrals to the point you want.

One of the best ways to generate referrals is simply to ask your customers for them.

Ask them to tell their friends and reward them for doing it.

You can follow the same type of plan you used for getting customers to come back.

Place offers in your newsletter, give them rewards for each new customer they bring to your business, make it worth their while to help you.

Not only will you generate referrals, but this will help your customers develop a feeling of ownership about your business.

Check out "Instant Referrals" for 21 more referral strategies.

Why People Refer Businesses

Once you understand what motivates people to refer your business to their friends, creating those referrals is far easier.

People love to tell others what they think.

They feel smart alerting others to good or bad things, they'll spread a message when it benefits them, they'll do it if their friends benefit and they'll do it when they care about the outcome.

But don't forget, people will also spread your message if you ask them to, at least most of the time.

People like to think they've found something special, no matter what it is.

Think about that rock band you loved before everybody else had heard them.

You felt like they belonged to you and because of that feeling you cared a lot about them.

That is how you want your customers to think of your business.

When they feel ownership, they will tell everyone they know about how great your business is.

And the best part about it is that people are far more likely to trust an opinion from a friend than they are to trust advertising.

When a friend tells another about something they really like, invariably that second friend just has to try it.

It's human nature.

Successful businesses take advantage of that element of human nature, using customer service and relationship building to generate both referrals and repeat business.

Fire Your Customers

Several years ago, Brad Anderson, the then-CEO of the U.S.-based electronics retailer Best Buy, started to segment his customers in a very unique way.

Seeing that the company's top 20% of its customers generated 80% of its revenue, Anderson started to separate customer groups into "angels" and "devils."

The angels, according to Anderson, were the "early adopters" of technology and were customers who boosted profits by snapping up HDTVs, portable electronics and any new DVDs at retail (or close to retail) prices.

The devils, on the other hand, were the retailer's "worst of the worst."

Of the 1.5 million customers who walked through Best Buy stores on a daily basis, the devils would only buy heavily discounted or marked-down products.

They were also known for applying for every rebate possible, or buying and then returning full-priced purchases, only to buy them again at cheaper, "gently used" discounts.

They also loaded up on every "loss leader" item they could find.

Some even turned around and re-sold those items on eBay – profiting on the back of the retailer.

Finally, the "devils" would surf the internet to find rock-bottom pricing, taking advantage of Best Buy's low price guarantees to force the retailer to make good on its "lowest price" promises.

While the top 20% of Best Buy's angels generated a majority of profits, the bottom 20% of the devils cut into profits, frustrated the team and made life miserable for store managers.

In Best Buy's case, at the time that meant a rough total of 500 million customer visits could be categorized in the "devil" segment.

What would you do if wanted to lop-off almost half-a-billion visits to your retail location next year?

Could you do it knowing you risked visit volume for the chance of higher profits?

Anderson and his team did ... gently moving those "devils" off to their competition, who thought Best Buy was crazy – and greedily leaped to serve them.

Five years later, Best Buy was generating more than $45 billion in revenue, while their nearest competitor, Circuit City, got caught up in the financial tsunami.

Chances are if you really look at your numbers, you will discover like Mr. Anderson that the 80/20 Rule really exists – and both lives and breathes in your company.

The numbers may swing 70/30, but the strategy you need to employ is the same regardless of the exactness of the ratio.

That means that your own customer base, even in a professional service firm, can be segmented by profit contribution to your bottom-line.

Just imagine how much easier your life and the life of your team would be if you focused your resources on your best customers? Imagine how much more profitable your company would be.

And what do you do about your "C" and "D" customers?

Sack them.

It's as simple as that.

Not only are they wasting your time and resources, they are constantly looking for bargains and discounts, price-cutting tactics that literally take dollars out of your pockets and profits off your bottom-line.

To get rid of them, increase your prices. For most of the C and D's, any price increase is enough to drive them away and off to your competition – where they will now be someone else's problem.

Second, you can quietly start to eliminate the pricing schemes that attract C's and D's – namely rebates and low price guarantees

Finally, you can train your team to be more forceful and protective of your price points and the service options available from your company ... remembering there is a difference between being "of service" and being a "servant."

You would be more than willing to fire an employee who wasn't living up to a standard or was taking from the company – wouldn't you?

You should take the same view of your own "devils" in your customer base.

Not only are they not living up to a standard of exceptional profitability, they end up costing you dearly in terms of time, effort and resources every time they walk through your doors.

Take stock in your inventory – this time of your customers – and start the process of pruning your way to higher profits and a happier team.

And there's no better time than right now to start firing the worst of your customers.

Chapter Review – "9 to Grow On"

1) There are 9 Basic Need of the customer. When you offer to fill a basic need, it's easier to consider and choose the best strategies to communicate that need to your customers.

2) Whatever system you put into place and decide to test and measure, it needs to address one (or a combination) of 9 basic human needs.

3) According to the "Pareto Principle" 20 percent of your customers will account for 80% of your business. Focus on your best customers and make them as happy as possible to ensure they come back to buy from you time and again.

4) The goal of your efforts should be to create "Raving Fans" who refer and recommend your company to others.

5) "Word of Mouth" advertising is the least costly and most effective kind there is. However, you need to have the proper systems in place to make that happen.

6) Start rating your customers by grades of A, B, C, and D.

7) Your goal is to work with only A and B customers, and give your C and D customers a reason to price shop and haggle with your competition.

8) Can you separate your customers into "Angels" and "Devils" to better understand which ones are worth keeping and which are worth losing?

9) When you no longer have to waste time and resources on unprofitable customers, you can devote your time to customers that serve your business as well as you serve them.

3 Things to DO after your Review:

1) Figure out which of the 9 Basic Needs your company fills and the best way to communicate that to your customers and potential customers.

2) Apply the 80/20 rule to your current client or customer base. How? List them all on a spreadsheet, then draw a line that separates your top 20% of revenue producers from the bottom 80%. Come up with 5 ways to strategically eliminate the bottom 80% from your business, and 10 ways to keep, retain and create effective referral programs for your top 20%.

3) Research some ways other companies have segmented their customer base. How can you apply those "real world" lessons to your company right now?

Chapter 6:

Ways to Boost Lifetime Value

Now that we've talked about the ideas of acquisition costs and lifetime value, let's take a look at some strategies you can use in your business to generate and boost the lifetime value of your customers.

What's the "model" for lifetime value?

First, in talking about lead generation, we're talking in terms of marketing.

When it comes to conversion rates and average dollar amount, the keys to lifetime value, we're talking in terms of sales.

But it goes beyond conversion rates and average amount per sale.

When we talk about lifetime value, we are talking about creating a loyal community built around your brand and customer service.

Think about the overall sales process for a moment.

First, you need to build a rapport, and ideally that rapport develops into a relationship.

Only after the relationship is established, do you start to get referrals.

Viewed this way, one of the most important things you can do is to develop deep and meaningful relationships with your customers.

Developing relationships with your customers is all about meaningful communication that speaks to, understands, anticipates and meets different levels of basic human needs.

But this doesn't mean you abandon your sales efforts.

On the contrary, it means if you if you want your business to flourish you need to put equal effort into both bringing new customers into your business and developing deeper relationships with your current customers to bring more balance to your "new customer" and "existing customer" scales.

Businesses must understand, empathize and meet some basic human needs.

The Blog as the New Newsletter

In the conventional world of business, newsletters were a great tool to cultivate the lifetime value of a customer.

They still are and the typical obstacles that kept most companies from producing a good newsletter (time to produce, cost to print, cost to mail) have been virtually eliminated by blogs or online newsletters.

Hosting a blog that promotes you and your business requires only some inexpensive set-up fees and your time to populate content.

The purpose of the blog is the same as a newsletter.

It is to give your customers important, unique or useful information about your company, any special products or services you may have or offer, any upcoming workshops or seminars you may be hosting, or any one of a number of other points of information about you that your customers can't get anywhere else.

We'll go through some items that should be in your blog or newsletter in a minute, but one thing you want to make sure you have on your blog is some form of lead capture, meaning a way for people to subscribe to your blog so you can capture their email information and stay in contact with them.

You can create an opt-in database of people who have expressed in an interest in your company … to which you can create a series of sales pieces in what's called a "drip marketing" campaign.

In this sample of a simple Word Press blog … note the "Subscribe to Updates" box in the top left corner.

How to Develop an Effective "Drip Marketing" Campaign

Once you have an opt-in option to your blog, you can then add that email to your leads data base, and create a series of emails targeted to that data base.

Each of the emails is scheduled to "hit" the data base at specific times (at least once a week) … highlighting a new link your base might find interesting, or with an offer for a product or service.

You can use this tactic in segmenting your current customers' data base as well, giving special email "deals" or packages to your best customers, or in announcing special closed door sales (which we'll talk about later).

Drip marketing is cheaper than sending out actual letters, post cards or newsletters, and the return can be substantial if you are offering true value, insight, added value products or services.

The key in this form of marketing is to "give value first," and that value can be in the form of actual value (special deals, select customer closed door sales) or perceived value (information about a new use for an old product, or an offer for a "free" sample of a new product line or service next time one of your customers comes in you store).

Where Newsletters Still Have Value

While virtually everyone is online in some form these days, some people are still more comfortable looking at information from their mailbox rather than their inbox.

A lot of that depends on your customer base.

If you are dealing primarily with an audience over the age of 40, you are probably better off going "old school" with an off-line newsletter.

Why?

Some people in the older demographics aren't as technologically savvy as you might hope … and there is still value in actually going to the mailbox and getting something personally addressed to open and read.

In addition, a sea change of costs and technology have whittled down the volume of direct mail pieces in recent years, so you aren't competing for "mail box" space to the extent you may have a few years ago.

Whichever format you choose, the "Target, Offer, Copy" model still applies.

In either format, once you have your target, "content is king."

As long as your content matches the needs of your customers and offers a way to solve or meet those needs and desires, you'll not only get great feedback and more sales from your blog or newsletter, you might even notice your work has gone "viral."

This means your blog posts are being forwarded to networks your customers belong to, or your newsletter articles are being shared among co-workers and friends.

Tips for Creating Effective Blogs and Newsletters

Step 1 – Get your target right.

Remember, "Target, Offer, Copy."

If you don't know who your target market is, or what their needs are, you're wasting time and resources.

When you don't focus on your target, you fall victim to "everyone could be and should be my customer," when you know from experience that's just not true.

How do you find out what your target market is?

Start asking some basic questions:

- Who are the people most likely to be interested in your products or services?

- Where are they?

- What are they most interested in? What do they want to buy?

- When's the best time to target them with an offer? For example, is an email send on a Tuesday more effective than a Friday?

- What's their age?

- Are they primarily male, female or a mix of both?

- How much do the people you are targeting earn? What's their average household income? What do they spend their extra resources on? This may sound harsh, but you don't want a customer base that can't afford to shop with you.

And don't forget, you want to send your newsletter to as many potential customers as possible, so, most importantly, you need to know how to reach them.

Step 2 – What's your offer, or what do you want to say?

Although a blog or newsletter has the benefit of keeping your name in your customer's mind, at the end of the day it needs to bring you more business.

That's why it's important to figure out what you are offering with every blog post or newsletter article.

Is it something of value that is real and tangible?

Is it good "how to" information about a particular product or service?

Is it just a holiday-oriented "hello" or "thanks for doing business with us" type of message?

Building a relationship this way builds on the idea of "giving value first."

People simply don't want to read ads and sales pitches (leave that to your competitors!) ... they want something informative and interesting, that EVENTUALLY leads them to a sale (or better yet) a referral down the road.

When you position content this way, you'll have a more receptive audience than if you just pushed out sales messages all the time.

Other topics could include:

- The unique history of a product and what to look for when buying it.

- Success stories or testimonials of people who have used the product or service to solve a pressing problem in their life or business

- Interviews with vendors or suppliers about how new innovations or technologies that could transform the way people do business or live their lives.

- Newsworthy mentions about new hires, new clients, any types of awards or recognition ... or even something "out of the box" but personalized like a great recipe for BBQ ribs or an anecdote about great customer service you may have experienced in your community.

You can also take the position of "expert" and orient your content as "how to" tips, strategies or tactics.

Half of being an "expert" in your field is simply transferring the knowledge you already have to others who don't know anything about your industry or category.

Do it regularly and you'll be surprised how your reputation as an "expert" thrives both within your community and your group of customers.

Step 3 – Actually writing your content

You've got your target market or niche and your offer and list of topics, now it's time to actually produce the content.

First, you have to name your blog or newsletter.

Ideally, the name of your blog will contain your business name or your name as part of your domain or URL.

For newsletters, a unique, different or even funny name can be very effective, especially if it's a clever play on words.

For instance, a men's clothing store had a newsletter called "The Well-Dressed Mail" … while a fencing company produced a newsletter called "The Steel and Wooden Post."

However, unique and funny only work in certain instances, and if your business deals with serious problems or conservative clients, you're better off going a more conventional route.

No matter what you name your blog or newsletter, remember to have some type of lead capture (for your blog) or your contact information (for your newsletter).

You should also include any guarantees or unique selling points you may offer.

How long should your blog be?

Blogs are great because there is no set format for how many entries you can create or how long they should be.

Generally, you should be updating your blog at least once a week, and when you're starting out, populating it three to five times a week can be an effective way to both generate interest and start getting the blog indexed in Google and other search engines.

Once you start, you'll discover you can write your entries at the beginning of the month or week, upload them, and schedule them on a regular basis.

How many pages should your newsletter be?

The two main questions to ask and answer when deciding how big your newsletter will be are:

1) How much do you want to pay to produce it?

and ...

2) How much do you want to say?

If you are sending out newsletter through the mail, there are some other things to consider.

For a printed newsletter, the most common size is just one or two pages, printed on both sides.

That's a basic idea, but it really comes down to choosing your articles and pictures, then working out the size of your ads and coupons.

Remember, the goal of your newsletter is to make money, not drain your funds, so keep it simple.

Today, with all of the professional quality designing and printing programs available for computers, the cost of your newsletter should be little more than buying a high quality paper to print it on and the labor put into it.

How often should you run your newsletter?

Whether your newsletter is hard copy or formatted to be sent via email, once every three months is a good baseline and can certainly work, but once a month can be effective if you have good content, good offers and something interesting to say.

If you run your newsletter less often than once every three months, you might as well not run it at all, because if you're not keeping in regular contact with your clients, they are no longer your clients.

Regular contact ensures they remain loyal to you and you stay in the front of their minds, which is why it's such an effective way to build lifetime value.

To use time most efficiently, have your team edit or write articles on a rotating basis.

This is an effective way to relieve one person of the burden and still publish on a regular basis.

Is there anything else?

You don't want mistakes taking away from your message, so be sure to check both your newsletter thoroughly before sending it out.

Once you've sent it, be sure you have appropriate phone scripts to support what you discuss in your newsletter.

You don't want to offer a sale in your newsletter and have your team clueless about that very sale.

You need to generate scripts in support of what you talk about with lots of open ended questions, and be sure to train your team on what is in the newsletter.

What things shouldn't be discussed?

There are a few things you shouldn't bring up in your business' publication.

These include pushing your moral views and beliefs.

Most of your customers don't care what you think about the rest of the world, they just want to know what you offer.

Offending them can mean losing sales and you don't want to run the risk of offending anyone.

If you offend anyone, they might not come back to your store.

If you don't write possibly offensive things, that's one less thing to worry about.

Another thing: you never want to do is put down your competition.

If you run a good, honest business there's no need to take a shot at your competitors.

Doing so makes people think you have something to hide.

Your newsletter is meant to be informative, so don't make it an ego piece strictly about yourself.

Rambling about your experiences or achievements is a sure way to turn people off because it makes for dull reading.

Finally, never ever carry out personal vendettas in your newsletter.

Customers just want to buy from you and get on with their lives.

If you are constantly ear bashing them about this person that's done you wrong, they probably won't come back.

What Other Things Can You Do to Build Lifetime Value?

Lifetime value is about having relationships with your customers and blogs and newsletter are two great ways to build that.

But there are other strategies you can use to move your customers up the loyalty ladder.

Here are some of them, but to get the whole list be sure to check out some of my other books like **Instant Cashflow, Instant Referrals** or **Instant Profits.**

1) Closed Door Sales

Closed door sales are a great way to show your customers how much they mean to you by giving them outstanding value that they can't get any other time of the day.

These sales are normally special invitation events that are only for your A and B customers.

Like with any other thing you do for your business, you must test and measure the effectiveness of closed door sales, but this can be difficult for two reasons.

First you don't know how well your sale is going to go until you actually run it for real.

Secondly, if you run a closed door sale, invite your entire customer base and it fails, you may not want to run another one quickly after.

If you run another closed door sale soon after, people may get the impression that your "special" sale isn't so special.

There are other ways to test and measure a closed door sale's effectiveness, but if you're at a loss for ideas, you may want to run ideas past a few of your best customers and see if they'd be interested or if they have suggestions.

For this strategy to be effective, you need to find out what can really make an impact on the appeal of your closed door sale so people won't simply forget and not come.

That's why you should talk to your most valuable customers beforehand and see if there is real interest in this strategy on their part.

The nature of these closed door sales is to make your most important customers feel special, so if they aren't interested in showing up, there probably isn't much reason to have one.

An extra benefit of closed door sales is that they are also great ways to move stock that has been sitting on your shelves for a long time.

You can also add some value by giving presentations or adding networking to the mix.

Imagine you are a mechanic offering a closed door deal on oil changes.

Why not invite a representative from the company you get your oil from to discuss the benefits of certain types of oil on certain cars?

Don't be afraid to give something away at these events either.

For the same mechanic, give away a lubrication hamper from the oil company or something else that doesn't cost you much and your customers will probably be very happy they came.

That same mechanic could do tie-ins with a local racetrack or other venues that appeal to his customer base to add some extra buzz to the closed door sale.

What to expect from a closed door sale

To run a truly successful closed door sale you have to understand what your aim is because if you don't know what success is it's hard to achieve it.

Most business owners tend to have unrealistic expectations.

They think 90 percent of their customers will come to their closed-door sales and they will spend big dollars.

In reality most closed door sales only achieve a fraction of those results.

On average, about one in five people will attend a closed door sale and about half won't buy anything of significance.

This doesn't necessarily make your closed door sale a failure.

You're still going out of your way to make your best customers happy, which is always a positive.

It's also important to remember that any closed door sale that makes you any money should be considered a success.

If you simply take more money in than you lay out, it was a success.

But if you want it to be a big success, follow these steps:

1) Send invitations to all you want there. Make sure these invitations

convey a sense of real excitement so people change existing plans to come to your sale.

2) Offer real incentives for people to come. You might want to include some loss leaders to get people in the door.

3) Customer service is still vitally important. If your team just stands around looking like they don't want to be there, customers are less likely to have a good time and spend.

4) Greet people warmly, help them find what they're looking for and make an effort to sell to them.

5) Treat these sales like a social occasion. You want people to come with friends, stick around to enjoy your refreshments and walk out with arm-loads of purchases and positive feelings about your business.

2) A notice that you may be calling to say, "Hi" …

You could also let them know about a new program you have called "Random Acts of Calling" … which is a way to let them know you might be actively seeking out your customers and asking them to come back by calling them.

Of course you don't want to be a nuisance to your customers, but an occasional follow up call to see if they were satisfied with your service never hurts.

If you've decided to send out your newsletter quarterly, rotating your customer list and calling your A and B customers every few months is a great way to ensure you are on the top of their mind when it comes time to buy.

Just remember to script any calls you will be making to your customers.

One of the most important pieces of information you'll need on that call is the knowledge of what they bought the last time they visited you.

Don't make the conversation too personal.

Keep it about your business and their satisfaction with your business, and give them the opportunity to make some suggestions or offer ways you can make their experience with you better.

A simple script to use when making these calls could work like this:

"Hi this is (your name) from (your company). I was calling to make sure your new (what they bought) was meeting your expectations."

After they've told you whether or not they are happy with their purchase you can either find ways to help them or tell them about some upcoming events or specials that might interest them.

Don't take too long on the phone.

Remember, you are trying to build a rapport that evolves into a relationship, and in most cases, you wouldn't want to propose marriage on the first phone call.

You can also use this system to make follow up calls to keep people generally informed about what your business is up to, keep your best customers up to date on specials and sales or offer them special items or discounts.

No matter how you keep up with your customers, you need to follow up because without following up you won't get the real feedback you need.

By just making a phone call to follow up you'll be surprised at the leap in interest and responses you get.

Customers have a chance to ask you any lingering questions you might have and it's an outstanding way to cement any relationship.

3) Keep them informed of your entire range of products

It may be shocking to you to find out how many of your customers don't know exactly what you sell.

For many businesses, just keeping your customers informed about the entire range of products you sell can lead to an improvement in the bottom line.

The frightening thing about this is most customers would probably be willing to buy more from you if they knew everything you sold because they are already comfortable with you and how you do business.

That's why you should inform all of your customers of your entire range of items.

Send brochures and catalogues and work pro-actively to get them to buy products they don't currently buy from you.

This is called bundling, and it's a great way to improve the average amount each customer spends with you per sale.

When you keep your customer base informed of your entire range, you should never run out of stock.

If you do, you run the risk of losing customers.

Customers want two main things from the businesses they buy from, a reasonable deal and reliability.

4) Deal of the Week

Consider featuring a product of the week.

Offering great deals on selected products each week is an excellent way to keep your customers coming back.

People love bargains so if you let them know there will be one every week, they'll keep an eye on what your business does and buy what excites them.

Most importantly, it's an excellent way of keeping in touch with your clients.

Bundling for Profit

On-line retailer Amazon is a great example of a company that knows the effectiveness of bundling.

Whenever you buy something from them they usually suggest other items you might be interested in based on your original purchase.

It may not work every time, but it works enough to be affective and help the bottom line.

For instance, if you buy a book about business on Amazon, there will be a list of dozens, if not hundreds, of other titles you might like based on your purchase.

---

5) Re-booking Opportunities

Re-booking your customers is very important, especially for appointment- based businesses like beauty salons.

For these types of businesses, simply put, you need to follow up a completed appointment by asking them to set up their next appointment.

Scripting is vitally important in this step, as you don't want to ask the wrong questions and scripting makes it a virtual certainty that your customers will come back again.

For a salon, when a customer is paying, the person taking the payment should ask when the customer will be back.

For salons, generally four to six weeks is the correct time frame.

That is about how long it takes for a haircut or coloring to grow out and by simply asking the customer "Can I schedule your next appointment for the week of…" you are ensuring repeat business.

Of course this is true for any business that relies on appointments, so don't be afraid to ask your customers when they want to come back.

Don't leave it to chance because if you do they may find somewhere else to bring their business.

6) Until Further Notice Offers or Opportunities

Until Further Notice deals work extremely well with consumable products or memberships situations.

Cable companies and internet sites use this strategy and it works well for them as well.

The idea behind this strategy is that you continue to deliver the product until further notice, until your customers tell you not to.

This can only be done when you already have the customer's credit card number.

From there you just charge the card every time you deliver.

Obviously there needs to be an incentive for the customer to buy from you this way.

That incentive can be convenience or a financial reward for the customer.

We see this all the time as cable providers offer early season discounts for pay-per-view programming to the customers who enjoyed the service previously.

Another example is internet businesses that offer membership for six months but then automatically renew that membership when the six months is over.

To make this strategy work you need to offer strong incentives.

Be sure to be clear on the arrangement so customers don't dispute it after you've charged them for several products.

This arrangement can be dangerous if you begin charging people for items they don't want, which is why you must be clear with your customers.

That said, no news is good news in this arrangement but you still need to monitor your customer's satisfaction.

7) A Program to Plan Future Purchases

If you have a product that is being constantly updated why not help your customers and plan their future purchases with them?

For example a computer store could set a date with you to discuss an upgrade for your computer about a year after you've bought it.

Upgrades are a great way to position this strategy with your customers.

In this day and age everyone is looking for an upgrade after they've had a given item for some time.

We see this type of thing with big ticket items such as computers or cars all the time.

People like to be up on the cutting edge and keeping them not only informed but already on the road to buying is a great way to keep your customers coming back.

Just remember to ask up front about any follow up call when it's time for an upgrade and be sure to keep in contact with these customers so no other businesses invade your territory.

8) The Introduction of Your Frequent Buyer/VIP Programs

This is the classic method of getting customers to come back.

Simply give them a card that gets stamped every time they buy from you.

You can offer something like every sixth purchase free or maybe a special gift on that tenth purchase.

Work out some reward that is generous but affordable.

If you give a weak offer, people will dismiss it.

To make this strategy work best, of course have a great offer that isn't easily forgotten and keep reminding your customers how close they are to achieving their goal.

You should also make it easy to keep track of your customer's progress in case they lose the card or whatever item they use to keep track of their progress.

If possible, keep all the records yourself.

This strategy is so popular that if you look in your wallet right now, I'd wager you'd find a frequent buyer or VIP card from some business.

Maybe the card entitles you to a 10th sandwich after you've purchased nine or maybe you get a free pair of jeans after so many purchases at your favorite boutique.

Without a doubt you already know and understand this strategy, so why not use it?

It's simple, easy to implement and, most importantly, it works.

9) Create and Distribute an Up / Cross / Down Sell Checklist for You ... and Your Team.

Up, cross and down selling are great ways to boost your average dollar sale.

Up selling is great when you have a basic and deluxe version of a particular product.

It works by selling your customers a more expensive version of the product they're looking at, based on its benefits.

When up selling it's important to explain how the more expensive model will better suit their long term needs.

To do it effectively you have to clearly spell out the benefits of the more expensive item, then put the price in perspective.

If it's more expensive now but will save money for the customers in the long run, be sure to let them know.

A cross sell is a technique that is used by many large companies.

It can be very effective when selling products or services that are used in conjunction with others.

A good example is selling a watering system when customers buy a quantity of lawn seeds.

A men's clothing store could sell a suit with a vast array of ties.

You can also cross sell associated products or services on a commission basis with another company.

Finally there is down selling.

In this strategy show your customers the highest priced items first and then the one just a little more expensive than they originally had in mind.

All of a sudden what they wanted to buy seems inexpensive doesn't it?

Rather than trying to sell only a higher priced item and, as a result, losing the sale altogether, you simply sell a similar product that fits just above their budget.

For down selling, wait until you are absolutely sure they can't afford the premium product, you might just sell the most expensive item each time.

At the same time, try and make it sound as though there is little to no difference between the two products regardless of price.

A strategy that is similar to add on selling is simply running through a checklist with your clients whenever they purchase a particular type of product.

This list should be prepared in advance and used with as many different products as possible.

For example, if customers buy a can of paint, run through the list to see if they need brushes, thinners, drop sheets, stirrers or anything else necessary for a painting job.

In this method, you show your customers that you truly care about what they are purchasing because you want them to have the best possible experience.

After all, who wants to get home with a bunch of paint and brushes just to realize they didn't have any primer, edging tape or even paint pans?

10) Train Your Team with Scripts

Training your team to be the best they can be is incredibly important for lifetime value.

The better your team is trained, the better service they will provide to your customers, which should lead to those customers coming back time and again.

You need to be sure to have a written manual spelling out what you do and how you do it.

You'll want to use bullet points and concise headings.

Start with workflow descriptions and begin with the most important or regularly done task.

From there, itemize each action or function that needs to be done and give a brief synopsis, followed by the desired outcome and what happens next.

You should also spell out how to handle any challenges that may arise.

Once you have good systems in place you need to concentrate on finding the right people to run those systems.

Of course if you already have people working for you, you have to find a way to mold and develop them to fit your plans and ambitions.

The Focus on Lifetime Value

Harrah's (which is now known as Caesars Entertainment) has developed sophisticated customer lifetime value models to predict the ultimate value the company could reach with each individual customer, a "rewards" model that has propelled the company's success over the past decade.

Harrah's has been able to add millions to its coffers through the cultivation of their "Platinum" and "Diamond" customers.

Harrah's is very good at understanding how far they can stretch their existing customers and still make them very happy. They have found a highly profitable segment of customers that they might never have discovered simply by going through the quantitative exercise of assigning customer lifetime value.

Harrah's found that high rollers are important to their business, but the steady casino player accounted for 40% of their total revenue and a steady stream of income year-round.

Then Harrah's set out to take that wallet share from the other casinos by instituting new perks for them.

The victory came about for Harrah's simply because, in assigning customer lifetime value, it had to ask three simple questions: how frequently does this person come, how much do they spend on average, and how much do I need to spend to keep them?

Ultimately, this exercise also allowed Harrah's to put an implicit value on its entire customer base - the so-called customer equity of the company.

Further, it allowed Harrah's to more fully understand what its company was worth.

The ability to quantify the value of its customers was likely important when it negotiated a deal for $90 a share in its 2006 buyout deal with the Texas Pacific Group and the Apollo Management Group.

When you hire new team members you have the advantage of being able to impress them, right from the start, with what you expect from them, what your rules are and how you expect to go about their job.

This is a great advantage for creating a company-wide culture.

Unfortunately, for existing team members, a huge shift in the way the company is run, (like the implementation of systems) can be a reason to leave and find another job.

Often they become uncomfortable and don't like the idea of having to move out of their comfort zone.

A great team is one of the most important assets a business owner can invest in because hiring excellent people only enhances your business.

It's important to remember that your employees play a big role in the "Cycle of Business."

In the "Cycle of Business", the owner supports the team, the team supports the customer, the customer supports the business and the business supports the owner and around it goes.

Does this apply to your business?

When you understand how the different aspects of the cycle are inter-connected, you can see why it's so important to train your team properly.

Can you trust them to run everything smoothly when you leave the business for a day?

How about a week or a month or even a year?

What would your business look like if your team ran it for a year?

If you're afraid to even consider the answer because you know it wouldn't be good, look in the mirror to find the blame.

No business ever hires the perfect employee.

Perfect employees simply don't exist before they are hired.

They are made by strong leadership and systems.

So, who are you hiring and how are you training them?

11) Build a Dream Team

If your entire team didn't come into work one day, what would your business look like on that day?

It is your team that your customers deal with.

It is your team that represents you both in your establishment and when they are out in the community.

So why wouldn't you take every precaution possible to ensure you had the best team you could find?

Unfortunately, too many small businesses don't think that way when it comes to hiring.

More often than not, small businesses hire people they know or family members without giving consideration to their respective qualifications.

It doesn't matter whether your business is a restaurant, real estate agency or IT company, you must have the right people to have a strong business.

A simple one on one interview after reviewing a potential employee's resume is not enough to find the right person these days.

Anyone can lie on their resume or be the perfect person for a short period of time.

Personality tests help businesses learn more about potential employees.

Group interviews before a one-on-one interview can also be extremely beneficial when deciding whether someone is the right fit for your organization.

Then, train new employees to do things exactly the way you would do them.

And try not to hire friends and family unless they are qualified or add value to the business.

Of course, scripting is a great way to ensure that your employees follow the same company line, recite the same message and give the same quality service to every customer.

Once you find the right way to sell something, why change it?

If you write down what works and you use those same words every time, you are sure to have more success than if you are hoping to find the right words with each customer.

Once you have the right words, you have to be sure your team uses those same words when they are dealing with customers.

Yes, every customer is different, but your objective is always the same, to match your products and services to the buyer.

Don't be afraid to have a script for every situation you find yourself in.

From answering the phone to saying good bye when customers leave, nothing in the sales process should be left to chance.

To ensure your scripting works properly, make sure every member of your team has copies of all active scripts.

You should also write your scripts in a way that they are easy to say.

Don't use a string of long words or try to sound to fancy or knowledgeable by talking above your customers.

Just ask open-ended questions in a conversational manner and you'll be surprised by the rewards you get.

12) Perceived Value Offers

One great way to seal the deal with new customers or ensure that customers return to your business time and again is to increase the perceived value of the offers you make them.

You want to do something that gives them the perception that they are getting a great deal.

Then you want to place a time limit on that offer.

This pressure should help them make a decision and more often than not that decision will be to buy.

Make sure what you are giving them is something they will value highly but doesn't cost you very much.

For instance, some car dealerships offer a free tank of gas when customers buy a car.

You'd be amazed how many people spend tens of thousands of dollars on a car because of $50 of free gas.

To use this strategy the right way, look for low cost products that have a high perception value, stipulate a time frame during which the offer is available and when it will end.

Finally, make the special something either useful or memorable.

Chapter Review – "9 to Grow On"

1) Increasing Lifetime Value is all about generating repeat business... and that requires putting better customer service programs into place.

2) Blogs are the new newsletter. But even conventional newsletters can still be very effective customer service tools.

3) The main advantage of a blog is the email capture function you can add to it. That way, you can build an opt-in email data base then in turn you can start to email market via a scheduled "drip" campaign.

4) Remember, "Target, Offer, Copy." Once you have your target, you can create specific offers and test your copy.

5) For you best customers, you can also add value with a closed door sale. You can even turn these events into unique networking opportunities or workshops.

6) You can even create opportunities to simply call your best customers to say, "Hi," ... and give them an opportunity to share how you can make their experience with your company better.

7) When you're aware of how long your average customer will buy from you, you can create programs to retain them as that "end date" draws closer.

8) Even adding a couple of additional week, months or purchases can have major positive impact on your bottom-line.

9) Remember value is in the "eye of the beholder," and can be both tangible and perceived. Putting limits on certain offers or adding "exclusive" copy can help boost the perception of "scarcity" or "rarity" – upping overall value for your customers.

3 Things to DO after your Review:

1) Decide if you want an online or offline presence, and secure what you need for your blog or newsletter. Think about your targets, what you can offer and the type of content you can use. Set a date for launch ... and start now to develop these important tools.

2) Think about what exclusive product or service you could promote via a closed door sale. Think about your best customers, how much they usually spend, and orient this type of event toward those people and what they want to buy. Think about how you can reach them, what type of offer you can make and how you can create an on-going series of events that begin to get a positive "word-of-mouth" reputation.

3) Consider some of those customers who have been with you a while who may be on the verge of switching companies or who have reached the end of their buying cycles with you. Are there other products or services you can offer them? Can you show them new ways of interacting with your company? Can you direct them to another company who is in a strategic alliance with you so you can at least keep them in your network? Sometimes, a simple phone call is enough to open up new possibilities of keeping "old" customers coming back to lengthen their purchase cycle with you.

Chapter 7:

Getting Their Attention

Targeted lead generation is almost like the show "Deadliest Catch."

If you've never seen the show, it chronicles crab fisherman who set their fishing nets off the coast of Alaska.

These nets are actually cages called "pots" which are placed in the water, on the seabed and connected to each other by lines.

The crab fishermen catch only what comes into the pot.

The pot doesn't move, constantly looking for new crabs.

Instead, the crabs come to the pots and are trapped and brought up to the surface.

This is a great way to look at how every business should be attracting customers.

If you put your pots in the right place and fill those pots with the right bait, you're sure to pull up pots filled to the brim with crabs.

Focus On Your Niche

Who are your customers?

If you're like most people you never ask yourself that question and if you don't even ask yourself the question how can you possibly know the answer?

To target the markets you need to succeed, you need to know the Who, What, Why, When, Where and How of your customers.

A marketing campaign is not like a tent that covers everything.

Instead, a campaign is more likely to be effective if you segment or use niche marketing and asking these kinds of questions is imperative to marketing your company the right way.

It's important to get the real answers, not just imagine what the answers are.

You need to ask customers what they want and what can make the experience of doing business with you better and you need to find the best ways to reach them.

You can do this simply by asking them questions when they come to your store or survey your database.

With your top customers you should consider calling them from time to time to thank them for their business in addition to finding out what they like and don't like about your company.

Business is never so healthy as when, like a chicken, it must do a certain amount of scratching around for what it gets.

Henry Ford

Who is your ideal customer?
What do they want to buy?
What are they willing to spend to get it?
What are added services or products they might be interested in?
Where do they want to buy, online or in a real location? Where is the best location to get the most foot traffic?
When are they able or willing to buy?
When is the best time to reach them with your message?
Why do they want to buy?
Why do they want to buy from you?
How do potential customers hear about your store?
How do your customers make their purchases?
How can you make it even easier for them to buy from you?
How do you get them coming back? How do you turn them into raving fans and advocates of your business?
How do you raise the average amount they spend with you each time they buy?

Once you've got the information at hand, it's time to start using it to your benefit by marketing to specific niches.

Segmenting

Businesses must target their marketing to each particular group that can use your services.

Eschewing segmenting in favor of marketing to everyone through one campaign is akin to marketing to nobody and it is how most companies lose money when trying to buy customers.

What makes segmenting even more important these days is the fact that creative niche marketing is easier than ever, thanks to the tools at our disposal.

There are many ways to connect with the niche markets you want for customers.

Direct mail is a strategy that has worked for many businesses for a long time, host/beneficiary relationships or strategic alliances are also very effective, but some of the best, and easiest, strategies involve the internet.

The internet, and its business-minded brother, social media. are among the biggest changes to marketing a business today because the internet has changed how businesses reach customers and how customers find businesses.

How McDonald's Markets to Niche Groups Differently

Advertising for McDonald's is everywhere. But if you look closer you'll see that they don't use the same marketing strategy for each campaign. Instead they use multiple campaigns designed to stimulate each of their niche markets. They segment their markets to make it easier to connect directly with each one.

There are commercials meant for the early morning work crowd that feature the company's ever-expanding line of coffee and breakfast. They market to children with Happy Meals and strategic alliances with movies and video games. They market to young adults through commercials that feature dance or hip-hop songs and they market to older adults with their new line of high-end burgers. They even market to the health-conscious with alternatives to the usual fast food fare.

McDonald's is everywhere, their commercials are everywhere, but each commercial is designed to bring a particular type of customer into a local McDonald's.

Attention-Interest-Desire-Action

In some respects, generating new leads can be broken down into Attention, Interest, Desire and Action.

You need to draw Attention to your product, raise Interest, build Desire and spur your prospects to take Action.

Businesses still need to hit each of those four steps through specific mediums that will deliver your message to the best possible customers for what they sell.

It's no longer the goal of businesses to try to capture everybody's attention because it's just too expensive and can't be done.

Instead, you have to focus on niche groups who want what you sell and design your marketing to appeal to them, using AIDA in the process.

For example, in the past a store might advertise winter coats for men in their local newspaper.

The ad would read something like, *"Don't be left out in the cold, get your winter coat at XYZ Store today."*

There's nothing wrong with that right?

Maybe 20 years ago there wasn't, but today that kind of ad will get you nowhere.

A ski shop, shouldn't want to waste time with customers who want to find a long wool trench coat.

They want customers who are interested in ski jackets.

A fine men's clothing store, doesn't want the skiers, they want professionals.

Depending on which customers the business wanted to buy, they would target their marketing specifically to those segments of the population.

It wouldn't make sense for the company selling ski jackets to advertise to every group.

They should only market to those interested in buying ski jackets.

Of course some stores sell all kinds of winter jackets, but their marketing should still be targeted toward specific groups.

In this case, advertising should be done in certain mediums that reach professionals with ads designed exclusively for them, while, at the same time, advertising to the skiers through different mediums with different copy.

The AIDA formula is one way to look at how to buy customers, but there is another formula: Interest leads to Inquiry, which leads to a Purchase which, with the right customer service, leads to Repeat Purchases.

These Repeat Purchases should lead to Referrals which will start the cycle over again with a new group of customers.

Through targeted marketing, relationship building, technology and social networks, businesses that market successfully are simply available for their customers to find through various avenues and mediums.

Today most people know to take advertising claims with a grain of salt.

They are immune to full-of-hype ads that overpromise and under deliver.

Instead, the consumer of today uses information and loyalty to decide who they will buy from.

Interact with Customers Online

Interaction is a great way and social media offers myriad ways to make your media presence interesting through interaction.

Some companies have games on their websites. Some answer questions directly or even offer special value to customers that interact with them.

Interaction is what social media is made for and it makes answering those questions about your customers far easier, so use it.

Smaller Can Be Better

Within the niche it's meant to appeal, marketing should be innovative and interesting and social media gives every business the opportunity to do just that.

Large, global corporations thrive because of the way they use social media in addition to their advantages in the world of traditional media.

According to one poll, people trust television advertising 30% more than they trust online advertising but production values of those ads play a big part in the trust factor.

Those polled believed that the higher production values translated into a more financially stable business which, in turn, made the ad, and the company, seem more reliable

Can you see where this might be a problem for small businesses that don't have the money to produce high quality television advertisements?

In traditional advertising, you have to go big or go home.

Television, radio and even print ads are expensive and if they don't reach the proper target, small businesses find themselves throwing money away.

Plus, it's very tough to measure return on mass media marketing and I believe that if you can't measure it you shouldn't do it.

Online Challenges

People don't trust online advertising, but there are options for online marketing that don't include popup ads or spamming and make it seem like you aren't advertising at all.

Online ads are often disregarded because they are perceived as a goal impediment.

If you've ever looked for one thing and dozens of ads popup, you know what I mean.

At the same time, it's also important to remember that the internet is far more goal and task oriented than television or radio.

It's also far more interactive.

This means it's easier to keep your customers engaged and generate calls to action on the internet than through traditional media.

Correctly segmenting and targeting customers are ways businesses make their online presence a destination for potential customers.

They focus on particular markets, making different offers to each group within their targets, and they offer a message that gives people a clear understanding of who the company is and what they offer.

The Educated Consumer

The world we live in is populated by educated consumers.

They expect a certain experience from the companies they buy from and they value service.

It is the business' job to create that experience and ensure the experience remains one that customers want.

This is the basic idea I've used to build my businesses.

The customer may not always be right, but without customers there is no business, so making the best of your customers happy must always be a priority.

You have to educate your customers about what you do.

You have to build relationships with them.

You have to continually cultivate your best customers' business.

You need to be specific about the products and services you sell, alert potential customers to what you do and make it easy for them to buy from you.

Learn Before You Earn

I am a big believer that you must learn before you earn, and learning, by its very nature, facilitates change.

Learning changes the way you see the world, and the more you know, the easier it is to see the issues that affect your business.

But learning is just the first step.

Despite the cliché, you must understand that knowledge isn't power.

Wisdom is power, and wisdom only comes with the application of knowledge.

If you take what you learn in this book and fail to apply it, did you really learn anything?
I will teach you how to buy customers efficiently in this book, but

if you don't embrace the change and apply what you've learned to your real life situation, it won't do you any good.

Your knowledge won't give you the power to achieve anything, only the application of that knowledge will.

The Ultimate Price of Finding Your Niche

How would you like to never compete on price again?

Easier said than done, I know.

But now is the perfect time to find the "sweet spot" in your business where you can compete anything other than price.

That "sweet spot" could also be called your niche, and when you find it and operate from it, you'll find business becomes a lot more fun and profitable.

My definition of a niche is pretty simple: a place you can operate with no price competition.

When you find a great niche for your company, price as an objection goes to the bottom of your prospects' and customers' lists.

In fact, companies with great niches soon discover they have customers who will go to great lengths to do business with them – many times regardless of price.

This is important because when companies continually discount and compete on price, they are not only losing the pricing game, they are also losing the profit game – and as so many companies have so recently discovered, without profit, the game is over.

So how do you go about finding your company's niche?

First, Find Your Own USP – Unique Selling Proposition

What is the one thing your company does that others in your category don't?

Is it a method of delivery? Is it customer service?

Or is it something else that uniquely defines your business, say your history, a unique way you manufacture your product, or an interesting geographic location?

Whatever it is, identify it, define and it and start using it to differentiate yourself in the market place.

Don't think that a "commodity" product can have a USP?

Just go online and look at how the grass seed company Scotts markets its "Turf Builder" line of grass seed.

Don't know if a "small" company can define itself against a larger competitor?

Pick up a copy of the new book about the U.S.-based In-N-Out Burger, which beats McDonald's in terms of overall profitability and same-store sales – with fewer stores and less menu items.

Wonder if you can profit in your small niche?

Take a look at Porsche, which targets a select few customers at a very high product performance level and price point, and in turn is one of the most profitable car makers around.

Second, Offer a Guarantee

While every business is required to make good on its products or services, add some extra value to your guarantee, and make it part of your overall customer experience.

For years, top-tier retailers have all had generous guarantee and return policies, and those policies have only strengthened customer loyalty to their stores.

Can you make your guarantee stand out?

Can it become the industry standard?

If so, start telling your customers and your prospects and start making it a distinction you can sell in the marketplace.

And don't worry about getting ripped-off with a strong guarantee. Sure, some will take advantage.

But in the end, your reputation and additional sales will more than make up for the single digit percentages that look to scam you or take advantage of your policies.

Finally, Market Yourself in Terms of Your USP

Once you identify your USP and get your guarantee set, start defining each in your marketing.

There's an old adage in marketing that if you can't find your niche, create a new one.

What this means is that it is always better to be the first in a niche than the second or third company in a proven category.

New niche makers and category leaders tend to be highly focused, and sometimes, that focus can appear too narrow.

Yet in the end, almost paradoxically, the narrow niche or category can grow precisely because it is so unique and different than anything else.

A list of the most valuable brands in the world features companies that have established themselves within their niche.

Some of those include:

1. *Google*
2. *Microsoft*
3. *Coca-Cola*
4. *IBM*
5. *McDonald's*
6. *Apple*
7. *China Mobile*
8. *GE*
9. *Vodafone*
10. *Marlboro*

With the exception of GE (which has been around now for more than a century, and to a certain extent IBM), all of these companies can be defined by a single word of focus in their niche – even if those niches are now worth hundreds of millions – or billions – of dollars.

The single word focus is something that especially true for the list's first $100 billion brand – Google – which is probably the most highly niche-oriented and focused of all the companies on the list.

Ultimately, of course, that is your goal – to find the one key phrase your customers and prospects use or will use to describe what your company does in an ideal business world.

You want people to say, "OH, you're the people who … "

Not only will your marketing efforts start to generate real results, you'll be able to compete on everything other than price.

You'll also find once you and your customers get price out of the way, you'll be a lot more creative in your added value propositions, your marketing and your customer service.

You'll also have much bigger numbers on your bottom-line.

Chapter Review – "9 to Grow On"

1) Buying customers means you have be "fishing" in the right spots, with the right "bait" … meaning something the fish want to eat.

2) The dictionary's definition of a "niche" is "a place, employment, status, or activity for which a person or thing is best fitted." It's also defined as a "specialized market." Either way, finding and focusing on your niche is the most powerful way to leverage all the resources and activities in a business.

3) You can leverage your niche by promoting certain features or attributes of your products or services that are important or desired by your customers.

4) Even if you have a large and diverse customer base, you can still find unique niche opportunities in your company by looking at what certain segments of your customers buy. Then, you can add value by bundling or creating special packages or products focused on these segments.

5) Large companies (like McDonald's) have mastered the science of targeting niches and segmentation. It's one of the ways they drive extra revenues in mature categories.

6) The conventional advertising mantra of "AIDA" … ("Attention, Interest, Desire, Action") is be better focused by simply viewing your lead generation strategies in terms of "Target, Offer and Copy." If your target is right, and you've got a good offer, the AIDA will take care of itself.

7) The "Purchase Cycle simply means Interest in your product or service leads to Inquiry; Inquiry leads to a Purchase, and Purchase should lead to Repeat Purchases. Remember, profit is made in repeat purchases or repeat transactions.

8) Today's buyer is more educated than ever, so it pays to start long-term relationships with them in new media, including online platforms and social media.

9) In business, you need to "Learn Before You Earn" … so it's important to learn how the numbers and processes really work so you can apply them in the "real world."

3 Things to DO after your Review:

1) Use the questions in the chapter to help you define and identify your niche. Once you do, see if others in your competitive set are offering the same or similar types of products or services. What do they charge? What do they do well? Not so well? How can you differentiate yourself from the competition? One thing to consider ... if you are carrying products or offering services no one else does and they don't sell very well, have you really found a new niche or simply a product or service no one wants to buy?

2) Take inventory of your last few ads. Do they fit the "AIDA" model? Do they fit the "Target, Offer, Copy" model? Neither? Both? How can you rework your materials so you are more in line with your customers, what they want to buy and the offers that are compelling to them?

3) Consider your own "Purchase Cycle" and how the cycle applies to your business. Are there gaps between an Inquiry and a Purchase? How long is the gap between a first Purchase and a Repeat Purchase? What are some strategies and tactics you can use to close them, with the resources you already have?

Chapter 8:
Building Your Team

Buying Customers is not something you can do on your own.

It takes the entire team, working together to build a strong customer base of "A" and "B" customers.

The next chapter explains the importance of having a good team and ways to build your "Dream Team."

Your Own Sales Force

Many businesses make the mistake of thinking salespeople are the only sales force, but everyone that works in a business can help generate leads by simply talking about the business with friends.

You see, everyone involved in a business should know how to sell the products or services that the business sells, but more importantly, every team member has a stake in the business doing well.

Because of this, don't underestimate the importance of including everyone on your team as part of your marketing and sales force.

Your team is the direct conduit between your business and your customers, both potential and current.

In that role your team plays a vital part in making your business successful.

It is one thing to have great people working for you.

It's another to have all the important elements in place so your team is a winning one.

How can you make sure you have a team that supports your vision of the business?

Let's take a look.

How to Build a Great Team (of Salespeople)

There are six keys that go into building a great team.

1. *Strong Leadership*
2. *A Common Goal*
3. *Rules of the Game*
4. *An Action Plan*
5. *Company Support in Risk Taking and ...*
6. *100 Percent Involvement and Inclusion*

You simply can't expect your sales force to transform your business alone.

You must train, script, encourage and reward them to make a difference.

There are many other factors in play, but luckily, most of those factors are controllable.

Ultimately, however, it's up to you to control these factors to ensure they compliment your team.

Let's take a look at each one of these to see how they can work for you ...

Develop Strong Leadership

Strong leadership is when people trust and respect you to unwaveringly support the direction in which you lead the business.

If your sales force and company team isn't guided by strong leadership with a clear vision and mission, the results will be like a ship with no rudder.

One of the biggest mistakes many businesses make is turning their top sales people into sales managers.

Selling products and managing people are two very different skills and businesses that do this simply weaken themselves in two positions.

Being a strong leader doesn't mean you have to be an autocrat or dictator.

In *Good To Great*, Jim Collins discusses how the companies he spotlights all have leaders who were more concerned with accomplishing goals and the general welfare of the company than their own needs.

The team needs to know that the leader is more interested in the success of the business than anything else and they have to trust the leader's vision.

No matter what style of leader you are, there are two types of behaviors you need to understand, task behavior and relationship behavior.

With task behavior, the main concern of the leader is getting the job done.

When a leader is involved with team members, telling them exactly what to do and when, how and where it should be done, that is task behavior.

Relationship behavior, on the other hand, has more to do with explaining, listening, encouraging and supporting team members when they go about their tasks.

Based on personality, some managers will concentrate more on task-related behavior, while others will be involved in relationship-related behavior.

Create Common Goals

Common goals are those in which not only does everyone know and believe in a given goal, but it's also a goal where everyone wins.

You simply can't expect your team to achieve results if they don't know what the overall goal that they are aiming for is.

There are quarterly goals, departmental goals and even big, hairy audacious goals, and each should be broken down into SMART goals.

SMART goals are:

Specific-Tell the team exactly what is expected of them. Leave nothing to chance.

Measured-If you can't measure it, how do you know when you've been successful? Measuring goals also helps because people can achieve smaller goals on the way to bigger goals, which leads to a feeling of accomplishment.

Attainable-We all know those people who set unrealistic goals and then are disappointed when they don't achieve them. If something isn't realistically attainable, it's not a goal, it's a dream.

148 Building Your Team

Realistic-Sure, you may want to play in the NBA, but if you are just five feet tall, that may not be a realistic goal. What can you actually accomplish? For instance, a new software company may not be able to compete with Microsoft, but there are smaller companies they can challenge for niche markets.

Timely- Have you ever tried to do something but it seems to never get accomplished? You just kept putting it off? How well did that end up working for you? Was it ever done? When goals aren't timely, it's easy to lose sight of finishing them or accomplishing what you expected.

Working with **SMART** goals helps team members achieve more because they know exactly what is expected of them and they have a guide map to complete their tasks

Set the "Rules of the Game"

Your team needs to know the Rules of the Game.

That also means you have to develop them and make sure they are followed and everyone is accountable to the same set of rules and expectations.

When you give your team a clear set of guiding rules, it's easier for them to get their job done.

More importantly, it gives any business a base of culture to work from.

For instance, at **ActionCOACH** we believe strongly in having a strong company culture.

That is why we created 14 Points of Culture that everyone involved with the company strives to live and work by. Of course no one is perfect, but clearly spelling out the Rules helps the team work together to reach their goals.

Here are the "Rules of the Game" we use at **ActionCOACH** and can help any business, which we call our "14 Points of Culture."

1. Commitment
I give myself and everything I commit to 100% until I succeed. I am committed to the Vision, Mission, Culture and success of **ActionCOACH**, its current and future team, and its clients at all times.

2. Ownership
I am truly responsible for my actions and outcomes and own everything that takes place in my work and my life. I am accountable for my results and I know that for things to change, first I must change.

3. Integrity
I always speak the truth. What I promise is what I deliver. I only ever make agreements with myself and others that I am willing and intend to keep. I communicate potential broken agreements at the first opportunity and I clear up all broken agreements immediately.

4. Excellence
Good enough isn't. I always deliver products and services of exceptional quality that add value to all involved for the long term. I look for ways to do more with less and stay on a path of constant and never ending improvement and innovation.

5. Communication
I speak positively of my fellow team members, my clients and **ActionCOACH** in both public and private. I speak with good purpose using empowering and positive conversation. I never use or listen to sarcasm or gossip. I acknowledge what is being said as true for the speaker at that moment and I take responsibility for

responses to my communication. I greet and farewell people using their name. I always apologize for any upsets first and then look for a solution. I only ever discuss concerns in private with the person involved.

6. Success

I totally focus my thoughts, energy and attention on the successful outcome of whatever I am doing. I am willing to win and allow others to win: Win/Win. At all times, I display my inner pride, prosperity, competence and personal confidence. I am a successful person.

7. Education

I learn from my mistakes. I consistently learn, grow and master so that I can help my fellow team members and clients learn, grow and master too. I am an educator and allow my clients to make their own intelligent decisions about their future remembering that it is their future. I impart practical and usable knowledge rather than just theory.

8. Team Work

I am a team player and team leader. I do whatever it takes to stay together and achieve team goals. I focus on cooperation and always come to a resolution, not a compromise. I am flexible in my work and able to change if what I'm doing is not working. I ask for help when I need it and I am compassionate to others who ask me.

9. Balance

I have a balanced approach to life, remembering that my spiritual, social, physical and family aspects are just as important as my financial and intellectual. I complete my work and my most important tasks first, so I can have quality time to myself, with my family and also to renew.

10. Fun

I view my life as a journey to be enjoyed and appreciated and I create an atmosphere of fun and happiness so all around me enjoy it as well.

11. Systems
I always look to the system for a solution. If a challenge arises I use a system correction before I look for a people correction. I use a system solution in my innovation rather than a people solution. I follow the system exactly until a new system is introduced. I suggest system improvements at my first opportunity.

12. Consistency
I am consistent in my actions so my clients and teammates can feel comfortable in dealing with me at all times. I am disciplined in my work so my growth, results and success are consistent.

13. Gratitude
I am a truly grateful person. I say thank you and show appreciation often and in many ways, so that all around me know how much I appreciate everything and everyone I have in my life. I celebrate my wins and the wins of my clients, and team. I consistently catch myself and other people doing things right...

14. Abundance
I am an abundant person, I deserve my abundance and I am easily able to both give and receive it. I allow abundance in all areas of my life by respecting my own self worth and that of all others. I am rewarded to the level that I create abundance for others and I accept that abundance only shows up in my life to the level at which I show up.

If you can't decide on your own Points of Culture, feel free to use these in your business.

Build an Action Plan

The fourth key to building a great team is your Action Plan.

This is when you give your team a clear plan of who does what and by when.

The Action Plan can also be considered the mission and vision for a given business.

What do you want to accomplish and what is the way you will get there?

When the entire business is on the same page, it's easy for team members to commit to what they have to do.

Telling everybody what your mission and vision are is a strong way to do just that.

Support Risk Taking

Risk taking is important for a number of reasons.

It helps develop the relationship you have with your team, empowering team members.

It brings in new ideas and strategies to the business and it makes the work of business that much more fun.

Not every great idea for a business comes from the top down.

Often, team members who see challenges every day have great ideas that can be very helpful and even profitable.

Good leaders support these team members and others that speak their mind and have ideas.

It's important to remember that business should be fun and support some risk taking as a leader helps in that department.

For lead generation strategies, the more empowered your team is, the more likely they are to speak highly of your business, which can bring in leads.

I've found it helps to support employees who are self-starters because they feel a sense of ownership and accomplishment in their jobs that spreads to other areas of the business.

It's the team members who never make mistakes because they do the bare minimum that tend to need more training than the employees who take chances.

And it's the team members who do the bare minimum who will never help your business generate a lead.

100% Involvement and Inclusion

Finally, the sixth and final fundamental to building a great team is involvement and inclusion.

Each member of the team is responsible for being involved and as the leader, it's your role to include any and all who are having trouble being part of the team.

Your team should be more than just the sum of the parts.

Together they should make a whole that builds and grows a business exponentially.

If you can follow these fundamentals, you should find building a terrific team far easier, which, in turn, should lead to generating more leads for less money.

Remember, while your sales force may not play a huge role in marketing campaigns they do play a big part in generating referrals and building customer loyalty, which in turn builds lifetime value.

The best way to ensure your sales force is giving you solid return on your investment is to train them properly and a big part of proper training is scripting.

Through scripting you can turn potential customers into real customers and build their lifetime value to your business thanks to targeted questions that improve customer service and, in turn, loyalty.

How to Train People in Sales

What do you need to do to ensure the best possible outcome from your salespeople?

Proper training of course, is the first step.

Remember, your business will only ever be as good as your employees and your front line salespeople.

To train them properly take the time to get them to watch videos, read books and attend seminars.

You should be willing to pay for all of this as it is an investment in your business, not a cost for your business.

To ensure your team is trained in the best way possible, get the training yourself so you know what the best books, videos and seminars are.

When your team has received the training, quiz them or ask them what they've learned so you know they've been paying attention.

Scripting for Any Business

A tire shop I worked with was able to generate leads but they couldn't convert them to customers.

I was able to boost their profits just by using a very simple script.

You see, one problem they had was they would get a lot of phone calls, but they had trouble bringing those callers into the shop to buy.

All they did was answer the questions asked rather than taking the opportunity to build interest and spur the caller to take action.

All it took was a few lines to turn it around.

When a team member answered the phone they thanked the caller for calling and introduced themselves.

Then it got interesting.

"Just so I can better serve you, may I ask you a few questions?" the team member would ask.

Of course, the answer was a yes, so the team member went on to some questions.

If the customer was in the database, they would say, "I see it's been more than a year since you got new tires. Is that why you're calling today?"

If the person was not yet a customer, the team member might ask what kind of car they drive, what kind of driving they do or how often they drive as a way to decipher what type of tire would fit their needs best.

Once these scripted questions got the ball rolling, team members were trained in moving to other scripted topics that would build desire and generate a call to action.

Use of Scripts

As we've learned, scripting is absolutely essential no matter what business you're in.

Once you find the right way to sell something to somebody, write down exactly what you said and then do it every time.

Most importantly, make sure your team does the same thing.

Every customer is different but the objective is the same, match the product to the buyer.

You should have scripts for everything from answering the phone to saying good bye.

Be sure to write scripts that are easy to say.

Nothing sounds sillier than a string of long, useless words.

Most of all, be sure your scripts have plenty of open-ended questions.

Of course you need to test and measure so you can change any scripts with a lackluster performance.

Now that we've set the stage, let's discuss some real strategies you can use to generate leads for your business

Chapter Review – "9 to Grow On"

1) Your real sales force is more than your sales people. It can be your entire team if you train them in the sales process, your company vision and script them properly.

2) There are six keys that go into building a great team.
   a. Strong leadership
   b. A Common Goal
   c. Rules of the Game
   d. An Action Plan
   e. Company Support in Risk Taking and …
   f. 100 Percent Involvement and Inclusion

3) Company culture is important, because it provides context to your company.

4) If, as the leader of the company, don't create the culture, your team will create it for you.

5) As a leader, you lead people and manage processes.

6) Part of any results-oriented organization if a process of setting and achieving goals.

7) Any goal process should be SMART:

   • Specific
   • Measurable
   • Attainable
   • Realistic
   • Time-bound

8) Scripts can help even the most inexperienced sales or customer service people build rapport with any customer base.

9) People can always build their own personality into the script, but effective scripts act as a guide with the message points you want your team to communicate.

3 Things to DO after your Review:

1) Think about your own company. Does it have a vision and a mission? Do you know what it is? Does your team?

2) If you do, how can you communicate it to your team and get "buy-in" from everyone? If you don't … when will you be able to get your first draft of your own vision, mission and points of company culture completed?

3) Take of look at the script included in this chapter. How can you adopt it and adapt it to your own company?

Chapter 9:

Strategies for Lead Generation

Now that we've set the stage, let's discuss some real strategies you can use to generate leads for your business.

Use Giveaways to Both Bundle and Add Value

While I don't believe in discounts, I do believe in bundling and using giveaways to add value to any business, both tangible and perceived, for the customer.

Giveaways are a great marketing tool, provided you don't spend too much on what you give away, while making the giveaway worth having for your customers.

There are some important rules to remember if you decide to conduct a giveaway to promote your business.

Say the owner of a bridal shop is looking to generate leads.

She knows that brides begin looking for the right dress up to eight months before their wedding and most weddings are in the spring.

With these pieces of information the bridal shop can decide when a good time for a giveaway, or a bundled package, would be.

Once you know when to try a giveaway, it's time to decide what to give.

Since there isn't much repeat business for a bridal shop and the average wedding dress sells for $2000, what can that business do to generate more customers?

This particular bridal shop decided to give away a veil with the purchase of a dress.

If the dress costs $2000, offering a relatively small giveaway is a great way to bring people in.

Say the veil costs $150 to buy, but only $30 for the shop to keep in stock.

The cost to invest in buying a customer is only $30, but the customer feels like they are getting great value because they are saving the perceived value of a $150 item … which also happens to be something they need.

Investing $30 to buy a customer that will spend $2000 makes sense, doesn't it?

If you were buying a stock or other type of asset, you would make this type of purchase all day long, knowing your ROI was northwards of 6,000 percent!

So how do you build value to your potential customers?

Again, it's a simple as asking basic, but powerful questions:

- Who is your "Target?"

- What do you or can you "offer?"

- What is the message in your "copy" and the content of your sales script?

- What are your numbers, and how will you measure results?

Of course your ultimate goal is to generate more leads and convert those leads to customers, but it's better and more simple for you and your team if they know where they are going, how they are going to get there, and what they need to do to make their results happen.

What Will You Giveaway?

No matter what you give away, you want to increase how memorable your business is to both existing and potential customers while promoting what you do, aside from generating profits that is.

Once you've decided on your focus, you have to choose what it is you'll be giving away.

This should be directly connected to what you are trying to achieve.

For instance, a delicatessen that is looking to improve the foot traffic to their shop could gave away a free knish because they are cheap to make and can be distributed to many new customers.

If that deli were to specialize in event catering, such as weddings, anniversary parties or bar mitzvahs, giving away knishes wouldn't make as much sense.

Instead, they would need to focus on other giveaways that would connect with the catering market so it was directly connected to what they were trying to achieve.

Who Gets It?

Next up, it's time to decide who gets what you are giving away.

Sometimes the giveaway is just for new customers, sometimes for lifetime, valued customers.

Sometimes it's for customers that buy a certain amount, like airline miles.

How do your customers qualify for the giveaway?

If you have different levels and styles of customers, you should probably be giving each unique group a unique giveaway.

Once you've answered those questions, ask yourself, how does your giveaway tie in directly with your marketing?

Hopefully when you give your customers gifts, they value them enough to not just discard them.

You want your customers to keep what you've given them for as long as possible and, most importantly, you want them to remember who gave it to them for just as long if not longer.

How Timing Plays a Role

How often will you use giveaways to generate customers or even keep your customers coming back?

If the average lifespan of a customer with a given business is anywhere from three to five years, depending on the business, it begs the question, why do those customers leave after that time?

Could you use giveaways to keep customers from leaving, retaining them longer and generating more lifetime value from them?

I'm shocked more businesses don't think this way.

It's really simple, if your customers leave you after three years, what are you doing four months before they leave to keep them?

You might offer free items to long time customers to get them to stay.

Planning your giveaways for this purpose, or to take advantage of seasonal or monthly opportunities, is an important aspect of this strategy and relates to what you want to accomplish, which is keeping that cash register ringing, so take the time and plan what you want to give and when you want to give it.

Tie Your Giveaways to Future Sales

One great benefit of giveaways is when you make them tie directly into your future sales.

You can do this by giving away something that requires future contact to redeem.

We see convenience stores do this all the time with free soft drink refills.

How many extra sales do you think those stores get when their existing customers just want to refill their 32 oz. plastic cup for free?

Do you think they might sell some extra candy bars along the way?

Another great method for promoting contact with giveaways is to send redeemable coupons to customers that they can use.

If a business targets the right group of potential customers and makes an offer of redeemable coupons, why wouldn't those leads use those coupons to buy something?

Groupon is one of the most popular deal of the day websites around, but does it make financial success for businesses?

Here's a quick case study of a restaurant that worked with Groupon:

- Business Type: Very Casual Dining
- Business Age: Fairly new business
- Groupon offer: $20 certificate for $10
- Groupon's commission: 50%
- Total Sold: 1,225
- Redemption Rate: 68% (32% were never cashed in)
- Average Ticket Amount (with certificate use): $20 (people spent pretty close to the face value amount)
- Estimated number of new, recurring customers: 75 percent. These are people that will come back even without a certificate.
- Estimated long term, recurring customer income: $20. Without the Groupon, the average ticket is about $10. This means that it is assumed the new, recurring customers mentioned are expected to come in about 4 times over the "long term."

The real world result is that this business owner was paid $6,000 with costs around $5,000.

According to their calculations, campaign profit was $1,076.52, total long term profit was $13,883.33 and their return on investment over the long term figures to be 130.77 percent.

Of course, there are some things worth mentioning:

- The business was paid by Groupon in three, equal payments over 1-2 months. They were happy with this, but will that work for you?
- Purchases with certificates with tickets less than $20 don't get change. Typically, customers would order something else to get over the $20 level.

- Redemption volume was heavy in the first and last month, the numbers were:

  o Month 1 – 225
  o Month 2 – 150
  o Month 3 – 100
  o Month 4 – 50

Unfortunately, the number of new, recurring customers is very difficult to determine through Groupon, and must be tested and measured. Remember, you have to know your numbers!

One strategy that can be used is sending playing cards to different groups of customers.

Their top customer might get Kings while new prospects get Jacks.

When these customers come back to the business to redeem their cards, the staff already knows a little bit about the customer and their buying history with the company.

Generating contact is an important part of the giveaway strategy because it allows you to put your other systems into action, generating more business.

Think about it this way, if you sent your customers those playing cards and they brought them back to your business to redeem, you already have a perfectly scripted way to begin talking to them.

You know if they've bought from you before and whether they have or not, you can speak to them accordingly.

Remember, building relationships is the key to building a thriving business, so take the giveaway opportunity to do just that, build relationships with your customers.

Next Step Strategy: Referrals

What is the best resource for generating more leads?

The answer is right under your nose.

The best way to generate more leads is to use the customers that already buy from you.

In today's world of slick marketing and advertising, people trust their peers more than they trust old-fashioned ads.

This is one of the factors that make marketing through social media so effective.

We will talk more about social media later, but at the end of the day think of social media as a platform to build and strengthen the relationships with your customers.

Referrals are the key to any successful business and if you can turn your top customers into raving fans of your business you have gone a long way to ensure the long term viability of your business.

Repeat customers mean repeat business, but they also mean much more than that.

People do business with people they know.

They do business multiple times with people they like, but they only refer businesses they trust.

When one of your customers trusts your company, what are they likely to do?

They will tell friends, who will tell their friends, who will tell their friends and so on.

And when your service is bad and you begin to lose repeat customers, guess what those customers will do?

Tell their friends, who will tell their friends and so on.

Referrals Build Trust

People are savvier about advertising than they've ever been.

Most potential customers have been conditioned through years of blatant advertising, to tune out a great deal of information and a lot of what people do hear they don't believe.

How many times have you seen a commercial that makes claims to good to be true?

What do you think about the company that makes those claims?

Working with client referrals takes care of all of that for small businesses.

There is an innate level of trust when customers find your business through word of mouth instead of advertising.

People like to have things in common with their friends and if your business is one of those things they have in common, it can pay great dividends for your business for a long time.

So how do you make sure your top customers are referring your business to their friends?

In recent polls, customer service has been found to be the most important reason customers choose businesses, but also the most lacking category for businesses themselves.

Too many businesses don't concentrate on customer service, instead focusing on discounts and generating new leads that end up costing them in the long run.

If you concentrate on the way each customer feels after they've done business with you and make sure that it's a positive experience for them, you can find other ways of offering value instead of discounts.

How to Make Referrals "Worth It"

Businesses must make giving referrals worth the effort for their customers.

Reward them for their efforts with offers and events designed exclusively for them.

Sure, some customers might talk your business up even if you didn't offer them any reward, but why take the chance?

Invite your top customers to participate in the growth of your business.

We all like to feel as if we were the first to discover something special, so why not play up on those feelings to instill a feeling of pride and ownership in your customers as your business grows?

You can do this in many ways.

Make special offers to customers that bring your referrals.

Invite them to events specially designed for them.

Maybe even throw parties for them or use strategic alliances to give them special items from outside of your business.

If a business can find a way for its customers to know each other and become friends, garnering referrals and repeat business becomes even easier because these people have something very important in common, your business.

There are literally hundreds of ways you can reward your top customers for not only their loyalty, but their referrals.

The only limit is your imagination.

Not rewarding customers and taking full advantage of the possible referrals offered is one of the biggest mistakes businesses can make when it comes to generating leads because it's like ignoring leads.

Your customers have friends who value their opinion.

Make that work for you and you'll see your customer acquisition costs drop like a stone making the business of buying customers that much more rewarding.

Alternatives to Buying a Database

Aside from simply buying a database, the simplest, most effective way to create a database is to build it from your existing customer base.

When you cultivate leads from your own database rather than one you've purchased you have the advantage of a pre-existing connection with those prospects.

Social media is a great way to build a database.

In fact, social media is really something of a misnomer.

Websites like Facebook are really interactive databases.

On Facebook, for example, just hitting the "Like" button can be very beneficial to businesses because it allows people who might not know about a company find it through their friends.

Reaching Customers Online

With traditional marketing, businesses go in search of customers.

With internet marketing, businesses don't search for customers.

Instead they let the customers find them by giving customers the ability to more easily find them.

The internet has changed marketing for the better because it allows businesses to buy customers for less.

When you really think about it, the paradigm has shifted.

Now companies with a strong online presence consistently find new customers at a higher rate than their competitors that don't have a strong presence on the internet.

There are plenty of online businesses that do well because they connect with people looking for products or services.

Sites like Angie's List make it easy for customers to find businesses that fit their needs.

Amazon recently introduced a "Like" button of their own to help show customers other items they might like to buy, while websites like Tell-A-Friend or Facebook allow customers and businesses to interact and share information.

For the most part the internet is a fantastic resource for potential customers to do their due diligence on any business they may buy from, but poor sites can be problems that lead to poor conversion rates and sales, or a complete lack of interest from potential customers.

Social media is the hot trend at the time of this writing, but the world moves so quickly by the time you've started reading this book, there may be some new trend for businesses to use.

The common denominator that most of these trends will share is the internet.

The internet is a world-changing technology, like cars, television or even fire.

Without fire, man would've never evolved as he did.

Like fire, the internet is a necessary and vital tool for the well-being and evolution of any business, but it can burn you if you don't harness it correctly and let it grow out of control, so be sure to monitor your sites and blogs and keep your content fresh and interesting.

I think back to the days when the internet was first growing in popularity.

Creating websites was ridiculously expensive and there was little to no return on the investment.

It's no wonder so many business owners decided the internet was a money pit long ago.

But it's important to remember that certain aspects of the information age are here to stay.

The internet isn't going anywhere, cell phones are only going to become more like mobile PCs and the switch from internet surfers to dedicated app watchers is already real for many consumers.

That's why it's important for business to keep their approach fresh, constantly looking for the new way to connect with their customers.

Remember, only the tools or applications change, the basics of business remain the same, and the most basic aspect, cultivating a great group of customers, is still about building relationships and you build relationships by developing trust with your customer base.

In the end, it still comes down to getting the customers you have to buy more than it cost you to get them to shop with you over a long period of time.

This is a big reason segmenting and developing offers that speak to the feelings and needs of customers in a particular niche is so important.

Using social media or interactive databases to do it makes it easier than ever before.

A New World

Remember those days when finding something you wanted to buy took a lot of work?

First you'd have to look up the type of business you needed in the Yellow Pages or some other directory.

Then you'd have to decide which company to use based simply on a static ad that was probably at least six months old.

Then it was a matter of hoping you were dealing with a solid business rather than a bunch of con men.

Sometimes you didn't know until it was too late.

Well things have changed quite a bit.

There is so much more information available to us through the internet, deciding which business to work with is far easier than it's ever been.

For small businesses, having an online presence, and especially a presence on social media networks, is a great way to connect with existing and potential customers without the concerns of outrageous costs while creating the buzz and word of mouth every business needs to thrive.

Creating the right type of online presence doesn't take more than some work and follow through.

Even creating a website to promote your business can be done by almost anyone thanks to websites that can create and host your blogs like WordPress.

There is no excuse for businesses to not have some sort of online presence these days.

If you aren't up and running online, you can be sure your competition is and because of their presence, they are building relationships with their customers.

Having a website is no longer optional for businesses.

Just about everyone you might want to do business with has access to the internet.

If you don't have a website today, you may not know it, but your business is already dying.

Keys for Online Success

First, hire a pimply faced kid who drinks nothing but RedBull and is practically attached to the computer.

Why?

What do those kids do all day?

They sit online.

Do they go out to nightclubs?

Only virtual nightclubs online and they've been living that way forever.

Hire a kid, tell them what you want your site to be and let them work their magic.

They know more about websites than you do and you can probably hire them cheap.

The second key is to have more than one website.

At **ActionCOACH,** I have over 1000 registered domain names.

Of the 13 billion dotcom addresses on the internet, my sites are listed in the top 70,000 for traffic.

We are doing something right, aren't we?

Next, remember content is king.

On actioncoach.com alone, we have about 18,000 pages of unique content.

I have articles on everything from marketing to team building to anything else you can think of that pertains to business and coaching.

I also have a pressroom that features press releases and other news items about my company.

You have to remember that the world has changed.

Reporters find stories by Google-ing and searching the internet rather than pounding the pavement.

You need your own working pressroom because it allows you to send out news about your company that is ready to be picked up by other entities while you control the content.

To generate all the content I need, I employ full-time content writers whose job is to turn out articles, blogs, webpages and press releases every day.

The final step to building a great web presence is to have a blog.

You need to write an article about your industry as often as possible and at the very least once a week.

Fresh content builds brand recognition and databases and they are great for search engine algorithms and creating search engine optimization for your business.

Search Engine Optimization

Search engine optimization, or SEO, is a simple thing to understand.

It is just how highly your website is rated when people search for a business that does what you do.

Basically, when someone types "florist" into a search engine, how high do you rank.

It is very important to rank as highly as possible.

If you've ever done a search on the internet you know why.

Very few people will search past the first couple of pages, so if you aren't listed there potential customers won't find you.

To get those types of high ratings you need to have plenty of content and you need to interlink your pages and sites with other pages and sites. These are the keys to rating high on search engines.

Once you've got a strong SEO rating, you need to connect with your customers.

To rate highly with your customers you need to have a site that is interesting and makes people want to return over and over again.

This is another reason fresh content is so important.

Once you've got people visiting your site you've got to get their contact information so you can add them to your database and one of the best ways to do that is by using squeeze pages, which are among the most innovative marketing methods developed recently.

You may not know just how beneficial they can be yet, but business owners need to understand that squeeze pages can be their best friend when it comes to capturing new leads.

Squeeze Pages

A squeeze page is simply a webpage that takes potential leads to free information or gifts while first capturing their lead information.

Squeeze pages are easy to understand and they can generate a lot of business.

One of the reasons they can be so effective is that you can put them virtually everywhere.

Squeeze pages can be placed on most social network pages, on your blogs, your main web page, even sites like Meetup.com and CraigsList can house squeeze pages.

Just include a call to action and something that leads would be interested in receiving in your squeeze page.

You can promote your workshops, private sales and other events and even offer giveaways.

Using the internet is just one way to generate more business for your company, but it is vitally important you jump on board now if you haven't already.

There is no excuse for businesses to not have some sort of online presence these days.

If you aren't up and running online, you can be sure your competition is and because of their presence, they are finding leads that elude you.

Find a Partner

One way to generate more leads is by partnering with other businesses in host/beneficiary relationships.

A host/beneficiary relationship is when you and another business enter into a loose partnership to help each other take advantage of all your resources.

This situation is ideal when you have a specific group you want to advertise to and there are already other, non-competitive businesses dealing with them.

This relationship works best when the customers think of the offer as a free gift from the other business.

They believe the business has gone out of its way to find this offer and pass it on.

Because of that they feel some obligation to take up the offer.

Host/Beneficiaries - What They Are and How to Use Them

When I first started **ActionCOACH,** I used a host beneficiary strategy to generate leads.

I went to the local community newspaper and offered to teach a free business building workshop.

The newspaper was happy to get the publicity and offer some extra value to its readers and I got the chance to speak to local business people.

But to invite the business people, I needed the newspaper's database of customers, which they were happy to give because of the work I'd done for them.

A host beneficiary relationship can help both businesses.

One business gets a database, the other gets extra value that enhances their relationships with their customers.

When used properly, this strategy can be a gold mine for everybody involved.

Host/beneficiary works best when you ask to promote yourself directly to customers of another business, a business that doesn't sell the same product you do, but meets the same target market you wish to reach.

To get the business you want to partner with on board, you could offer a gift voucher through the other business, offer to pay for the business owner's mail-out, offer the business owner commission on any sales or simply offer the favor in reverse.

This can work exceptionally well for almost any business and offers the added benefit of networking with other business owners and developing relationships with businesses that have customers who fit your target market.

Sometimes host beneficiary is referred to as strategic alliances, but there are some differences, the most striking being length of time.

A host beneficiary relationship is generally a one- time or short term commitment, while strategic alliances can last a long time, sometimes years.

Strategic Alliances

Strategic alliances are relationships in which customer databases are shared and they last longer than a host beneficiary relationship.

To use either strategy correctly, you have to be sure there is synergy between the two businesses, because if your two customer bases don't fit, the strategy won't work.

For a new, chic clothing boutique, a host/beneficiary or strategic alliance with a hot hair salon would make sense, while partnering with the local boxing gym wouldn't.

You should try to create a win/win situation in these strategies.

Most importantly, once you've started using host/beneficiary or strategic alliances, test and measure your campaigns so you know what works and what doesn't.

Direct Mail

Direct mail is a way of advertising in which advertisers mail printed ads, letters or other solicitations to large groups of consumers.

Bulk-mail rates are used to lower the cost of the mailing, and targeted mailing lists are used to maximize potential response.

Direct mail is used in many different situations, limited primarily by the imagination of the business.

Stores typically use direct mail to advertise new products or reach new customers through coupons.

To create a direct mailing, businesses should work to create something that will appeal to a substantial number of people within their target.

They will then send it to a large group of people, depending on the potential audience of the advertisement.

That could be a ZIP code, a particular demographic or even an entire nation of potential customers.

Direct mail is appealing for a number of reasons.

It takes the message directly to the consumer.

While consumers might walk away from a television ad or flip past a newspaper ad, they will eventually open their mailbox.

Customers receive the mail at home, which puts the message in the hands of the consumer at the time the consumer might be likely to read it.

Direct mail is not without its problems.

Over the years, direct mail also became known by another name: junk mail.

Some consumers became irritated at receiving numerous ads in the mail each day.

Many throw away the suspected ad-filled mail.

This is a challenge to any business that uses direct mail to generate leads, but some direct mail marketers now use a variety of techniques to ensure that the recipients open their envelope.

Some will go to great lengths to make the envelope and mailing appear personal, even using special fonts that look like handwriting.

Others will target the mailing to the most-likely customers by using targeted mailing lists.

Many businesses that use direct mail have realized that one of the biggest challenges can be getting the reader to simply open the envelope and read the advertisement.

Direct mail has entered the world of the internet, and many of the same techniques are showing up electronically in email, as we discussed earlier.

Businesses are taking advantage of the relatively low cost of obtaining a long list of email addresses and the little time needed to mail to thousands or millions of people.

Perhaps not surprisingly, many computer users react by deleting what they perceive as "junk email."

Spamming doesn't work, but sending updates or newsletters online about your business does work.

Just be sure not to cross over to spam if you try an online direct mail strategy.

To ensure you won't be viewed as spam, give the people you send emails and newsletter to via the internet an opt-out option.

Story

Does your business have a unified message, a clear story?

Having a story and a message helps clarify exactly who you are and what you do, making it easier for potential customers to find you when they are looking for something in particular.

Sometimes just telling part of your story is effective.

Think about all of those businesses that have "Since 1977" or something like it printed all over their literature.

Or how about restaurants that tell you exactly how they got where they are today with a synopsis of who they are on their menu?

There are lots of different ways to get your story out into the public eye.

Use press releases, send out newsletters or even engage potential customers through storytelling by way of social media.

Offers

The most important questions to consider when crafting your offer are what and why.

What does someone want to buy and why do they want to buy it?

Once these two questions are answered, writing a strong offer becomes second nature.

For example, if you own a hardware store you probably have plenty of customers who want to buy a drill.

But you have to understand that it isn't really a drill they want.

It's the hole the drill makes that your customers desire.

The drill is just the tool used to produce the desired outcome.

This is true for any business.

It's even true in my business.

Few people actually want a Business Coach, but every business owner wants more profits while working less.

My business is just the drill that creates the hole.

Once you understand the nature of the offer and what people are really looking to buy, you're well on your way to building a great campaign, so what is it that people really want to buy from you?

Generating leads and turning them into lifetime customers is as easy as remembering that if your product is the fastest and best way to accomplish something, people will buy from you so long as you are targeting the correct market and creating the right offer.

Directories

When it comes to using directories to buy more customers, you are going to find a mixed bag.

Professional directories, or business to business directories, are especially effective ways of targeting particular groups of people because, in general, these directories are only viewed by people who already have interest in that particular field.

This works for businesses that makes things other businesses use.

For example, Boeing wouldn't advertise in traditional methods, or even newer methods. Instead, what can be purchased from Boeing, (meaning jets and the like), is advertised exclusively to companies that can buy from them, like airlines.

Can you imagine the "powers that be" at Southwest Airlines looking through newspaper ads to find a jet to buy?

For smaller businesses, business to business directories can be effective if your products aren't made for the public.

For instance, if you manufacture and sell medical equipment, you wouldn't market your products to the patients that need them, you'd market to the hospitals and doctors that use them through a professional directory.

Of course there are other directories to consider, like public directories.

Phone Directories

When businesses advertise through the Yellow or White Pages, or some other public phone directory there are some issues to consider.

The Yellow Pages are excellent for some products, especially the types that people buy only occasionally.

The Yellow Pages will work for you as long as you realize statistics show that more than 35 percent of people turn to the Yellow Pages when they're ready to buy.

Also their own statistics show response increases in ad size or Unit Display size.

When it comes to the Yellow Pages, the most important thing is to stand out.

Do something different than what everybody else is doing.

Remember, Yellow Pages readers are already buyers, they're just deciding who they should buy from.

On average, these prospects will call three other businesses before making a decision, which is another reason you should advertise in more than just the Yellow Pages.

For any Yellow Pages campaign, run a benefit-filled headline and use a photo rather than a line drawing.

Use key words so people know what you do and make sure your phone number is big and in the bottom right hand corner and, as always test and measure.

The White Pages are underrated by businesses.

Sure you can't advertise, but it's still another place that people can find you.

You should go for a bold heading so you're easily seen and make sure to list as many phone numbers as you can and in as many directories as possible.

Since the White Pages are nation-wide, it could be a good idea to put your business in as many of them as possible.

Other, less known, phone directories are generally a risky proposition, as the Yellow and White Pages are established as the standard.

Before deciding to use another directory do your due diligence and find out how it works for people that are currently advertising in that directory.

Remember, when working with any type of directory consider how many sales you need to pay for the listing.

I believe you should take reasonable gambles, but if it doesn't make financial sense it isn't a gamble, it's a money pit.

Follow Up

The follow up is a very important step in the process that should not be overlooked.

Being skilled at follow up can help in many different ways, including the fact that to follow up properly you need to compile a database of your customers.

This database alone can help your business incredibly.

This is one part that many business owners simply forget or ignore because they don't think it can work, but simply asking customers to come back is a very powerful way of generating repeat business.

There are many ways businesses can ask their customers back, including simply asking them to come again after they've completed their purchase.

Saying "come again" is a good start, but there are so many ways to invite customers back, finding the best way for your business should be relatively easy and far more effective than niceties at the end of the sale.

The Key to All Success: Test and Measure

The basic component of inviting your customers back is having a strong relationship with them.

After all, to truly invite them back you need to know how to contact them and nobody wants to give contact information to strangers.

I believe that to be successful in business, you have to enjoy it.

Of course, you need to work hard, but if you aren't having fun, work can feel like a drag and if it feels like a drag it's harder and harder to be motivated and moving forward.

That said, the most important aspect of any type of marketing campaign is also the most amount of work, testing and measuring.

Testing and measuring is not easy, which is why so many people hate doing it.

But just like that broccoli you hated when you were a kid, but your mother made you eat anyway, testing and measuring is the key to growing your business healthy and strong.

Test and Measure or Fail

Even the top marketing gurus in the industry make mistakes.

The Gap, one of the top retail companies in the world, changed their logo from one that was synonymous with their brand, to one that people simply didn't like.

After a short time and a number of complaints about the new logo, The Gap changed back to their tried and true, blue box logo.

If they had tested and measured correctly, they never would have had the problems with their new logo.

There are so many examples of businesses failing to test and measure to their detriment that we should go back to one of the most blatant and well-known examples, when Coca-Cola almost destroyed its entire brand by introducing "New Coke" in the early 80's.

Simply put, the crew over at Coca-Cola did not do nearly enough testing and measuring to see if their new product would be a success.

When it wasn't, they had to scramble to get "Coke Classic" back on the shelves before they had completely destroyed their market share.

Like The Gap, they failed to understand the power of testing and measuring and almost paid a dear price.

Today there aren't a lot of people that even remember "New Coke," which is a sign of the marketing power of the company.

But if they had correctly tested and measured their new product before releasing it, it might have saved them millions of dollars.

Don't Leave Your Business to Chance

Without testing and measuring everything you do, you are leaving too much to chance.

What you think may be good ideas may, instead, be leading your company to ruin, while ideas you think would go nowhere may be exactly what you need.

This is a hard concept for many business owners to understand, but you must always remember that you don't know everything.

There are literally millions of successful ideas out there that some very smart person wanted nothing to do with and turned down. That's okay. Not everyone can read into the future.

But what everyone can do is take the time to aptly test and measure every money making concept that comes out of your business.

Testing and measuring is the key to any successful business because nothing should be left to chance.

If you don't test and measure, you'll never know what really works and what is burning your resources. Failing to test and measure can be the reason a business is suffering and not growing.

Using the Strategies

From referrals to host beneficiary to follow up calls and postcards to your customer base each of the strategies detailed in this chapter can pay big dividends for businesses willing to use them.

It is important to remember that you want to use as many strategies as possible to ensure your marketing will reach the market you want to target.

Of course buying the customers is just the first step.

Next you have to make sure that the customers you generate don't just buy from you once but buy from you over and over again over the course of time.

How to Create a Referral-Based Business

In the business-to-business world, referrals are like gold.

In the retail world, referrals are even more important, because nothing is more valuable or cost effective to a retailer than "word-of-mouth advertising."

Over time, relying on referrals will not only turn your company into a more profitable business, it will shift costs and resources away from conventional marketing strategies into more personalized and cost-effective methods.

So how do you create a profitable referral-based business?

First, you need to decide if a referral-based model is the right model for your business.

While referral strategies work for any business, they are best suited for companies that sell higher-priced products or services, and are less successful for quick service restaurants or certain types of higher-volume categories like convenience stores.

The key to any referral strategy is the knowledge of who your ideal target market and "core" customer is, or who they could be.

If you want to shift your business to go after a new segment or niche, this is vitally important, because you will find that the more detailed you make your "ideal" customer, the more likely you'll be able to target that person for your business.

Next, you need to know exactly what you can offer, not only in terms of product and service, but "experience."

Look at it this way.

If you are building your business around "fast service" but your customers experience slow delivery times, you'll never be able to build a credible, consistent or effective referral campaign.

Finally, you need to work out what your costs are to buy a new customer and bring that customer into your business.

Knowing that number, however, is a base.

You also need to know how much you are willing to spend to bring your ideal customer into your business.

This is your new marketing budget, and the idea over time is to reduce the amount you pay to keep buying new customers.

So, what do you need to do with this information?

1) **Go to your current database and find who fits your "ideal" customer profile.**

What do these customers look like?

They are customers who:

- Pay on time
- Are pleasant to deal with
- Are happy to pay listed and/or quoted prices
- Are happy to refer friends and associates
- Are regular visitors
- Spend a lot of money with your company
- Upgrade on a regular basis
- Make use of after-sale services
- Are happy to be on my mailing list
- Are "Raving Fans"

2) **Once identified, segment the top 20% into A and B categories.**

3) **Communicate with all of your segments about your products and services.**

4) **Offer a gift, gift check, special pricing or some other incentive for each referral.**

Defining your ideal customer, segmenting your current customers and offering back a gift or "thank you" equal to the cost of buying a new customer is one of the quickest and easiest ways to start a referral-program.

It is also one of the best first steps to turning your business into a referral-based company and to reduce your overall marketing costs.

Start today and you'll be pleasantly surprised how your business had changed a year from now – and I would wager any amount that change would be for the better.

Chapter Review – "9 to Grow On"

1) Giveways and bundling products and services are a simple way to leverage your resources to add value.

2) Understand that timing plays a role in every lead generation strategy you use.

3) Tie your giveaways to future sales so you aren't just spending resources, you're investing them.

4) People trust their peers more than advertising, so use referrals to generate leads as much as possible.

5) Remember the principle of "What's In It For Me" when it comes to referrals. Make it worth your customers' efforts to send you referrals.

6) There are a number of strategies for lead generation. The key for your business is to test and measure those you think will work, and continue to actually use the ones that do.

7) Buying customer databases are easy ways to get new leads, but you can use your own database to cultivate leads as well, for a fraction of the cost.

8) You can use on-line strategies to stay in touch with your customers and generate new customers.

9) Host Beneficiary relationships (short-term) and Strategic Alliances (long-term) are great ways to leverage your lead generation strategies. Find a fit with a complementary business in your area and test and measure to see if your short-term strategies can turn into long-term alliances.

3 Things to DO after your Review:

1) Aside from traditional advertising, what have you done to generate leads for your business? Think of 5 strategies that you have used or are interested in using.

2) Think of potential Host Beneficiary or Strategic Alliance partners in your community. How could you market their product or service to your data base? How could they market yours?

3) When working with another business, start by offering value first and go to them offering a test to your own customer base, and you'll find more receptive partners to market your products or services to their clientele.

Chapter 10:

Strategies for Conversion Rates

Up to this point, we've discovered the key to increasing the Lifetime Value of your customers is to create great customer service programs, and to increase lead generation, you need to focus on creating tested and measured marketing programs.

Now it's time to move on to some strategies to improve conversion rates and average dollar sale.

While these are two different drivers of the "Five Ways," when it comes to increasing your conversion rates, you need to focus on increasing the effectiveness of your sales process and average dollar sale plays a part.

Look at it this way: Your marketing gets new customers in the door, your customer service keeps them, but your sales process has to convert leads into customers – or else you won't have any customers to keep.

Go back and look at the "5 Ways" and you'll see "Conversion Rate" and "Average Dollar Sale" are two of the driving factors that multiply profits.

You'll also remember most companies vastly overestimate what their conversion rate really is, while average dollar sale is a pretty easy number to understand.

Armed with the knowledge of what those numbers really are, especially conversion rate, you can immediately work on upping those numbers, which in turn will start to multiply results on the bottom-line.

Let's focus on conversion rates for now.

Most conversion strategies are pretty simple, and can be immediately put into place.

From a guarantee to scripting, these strategies have proven to increase the average company's conversion rates in every instance they've been tried, so you can only benefit by implementing them in your own sales process.

Let's take a closer look.

Why Guarantees Help Your Conversion Rates

Guarantees are powerful because they help take the risk out of the buying decision for the customer.

While guarantees help remove risk, the best guarantees focus on the average customer's key frustrations in buying from a company in your industry or category.

To have a really effective guarantee, simply pick the one or two things that your customers fear or see as a frustration when buying from you.

Then, offer to refund their money or put things right in some way that is satisfying to customers who aren't satisfied with service or the performance of the product or service you're selling.

Once you've finalized what your guarantee will be, it can be a selling point in itself.

Think about large retailers like L.L. Bean, who have built a legendary reputation and business on the back of their guarantee.

Retailers like QVC or HSN have also gone to great lengths and expense to guarantee to cover shipping costs back to the company for customers who don't like the items they've purchased.

However you structure your own guarantee, remember it is just one way to remove a barrier (in this case risk) for customers to do business with you, and in turn can be used as a "Unique Selling Proposition" in your own sales process – especially if your competitors don't offer a guarantee.

Guarantee What Matters

There are a number of issues people have with plumbers that have nothing to do with their actual performance.

Often plumbers aren't on time or they make a mess and leave without cleaning up after themselves.

Some customers are even bothered by the ill-fitting pants many plumbers wear.

So in response to these issues, this particular contractor made a few guarantees to their customers.

First, if you set an appointment for a given time, that's when the plumber will be there.

Second, this company guarantees that their plumbers will clean up when they are done.

They wear plastic "shooties" over their boots and even use a handheld vacuum to make sure the place is as they found it.

> Finally, this company also guaranteed their plumbers would wear belts, to keep those ill-fitting pants from being a problem.
>
> Notice this company didn't guarantee service, it guaranteed that people would not deal with common problems they might usually find with plumbers.
>
> And guess what?
>
> This business' market share has skyrocketed since making these guarantees.

More on "Unique Selling Points" or USP's

We've discussed the importance of finding a niche for your product or service, or offering certain products or services to specific segments in your customer base.

In the old days of mass marketing, a "one size" fits all approach worked.

But in today's flat and fast-paced world, the key to getting attention is to find your point of difference, and sell that difference as a competitive advantage to your customers.

One caveat on this is to make sure your USP is ANYTHING but being the low-cost provider or the discounter in your category.

Discounting simply means you will discount yourself out of business, and the only retailer I know of successful at this (Walmart) has such a low cost base as a result of its volume that few (if any) large retailers can ever hope to move it from its "Low Prices" USP.

While that's great for Walmart, unless you are moving literally billions of dollars of volume through your company, you're probably not going to get the supplier deals that Walmart does.

Better to focus on something other than price – so you can raise your prices – as your own USP.

The "Costs" of Discounting

Sales	Discount	Sales Price	Gross Sales – Net Cost = Profit
10	0%	$10,000	$100,000 - $70,000 = $30,000
10	10%	$9,000	$90,000 - $70,000 = $20,000
15	10%	$9,000	$135,000 - $105,000 = $30,000
20	15%	$8,500	$170,000 - $140,000 = $30,000

Discounting takes a toll on profits. As a 15% discount, a business not only has to sell more units to keep profits level, it's costs increase. The result? More work for less profit.

Why You Should NEVER Discount

"Never discount" is one of the things I always counsel, and the main reason is that whenever you do, you are literally stealing from the bottom-line … and yourself.

When you discount, you are essentially setting your business and your team up to work more for less money.

Here's how.

Let's say we have a company that sells water pumps, with a fairly high price point of $10,000 per unit.

Let's also say the net cost per pump is $7,000.

Whenever we sell a pump, our net profit on each pump, would be $3,000.

For example: $10,000 - $7,000 = $3,000

If we sold ten pumps at full price, our net profit would be $30,000.

For example: 10 units X $10,000 = $100,000
$100,000 - $70,000 = $30,000

Now let's say we decided to have a sale on our pumps, with just a 10% discount offer.

After our sale of 10 pumps at $9,000, we have a total revenue/turnover of $90,000.

Our net cost for ten pumps remains constant at $70,000, but our net profit has decreased to only $20,000 compared to our $30,000.

For example: 10 units X $9,000 = $90,000
$90,000 - $70,000 = $20,000

That doesn't seem too bad.

Until we realize we need to sell 20% more pumps just to keep our profit dollars "even" at $30,000!

Take a look:
15 units X $9,000 = $135,000
$135,000 - 105,000 = $30,000

The numbers look worse the more we discount.

At a 15% discount, we'd have to sell 100% more units to keep our profits at $30,000.

Example: 20 units X $8500 = $170,000
$170,000 - $140,000 = $30,000

So what can you look at to define what makes your company different or unique?

Ask yourself, "Are you the leader in your industry or category?"

For **ActionCOACH**, our USP is, "The World's Number One Business Coaching Firm."

If you're number one, there's nothing wrong in using it to anchor your sales messages.

- Is your product or service unique?

- Is the history of your company unique?

- Are your processes or procedures different?

- Do you have a geographic advantage over your competition?

All of these should prompt some thought and some answers about your company's own point (or points) of difference.

You can also look to focus on (as these larger companies have done) on the following:

- Customer Experience (Westin Hotels)

- Premium pricing and performance (Porsche)

- Service (Nordstrom)

- Delivery (FedEx)

- Speed (Google)

- Convenience (7-11)

To get started, list all of the attributes you can think of, then simply ask some of your best customers, "What are the main reasons you do business with us?"

Remember, the more you can align your points of difference with what is important to your customers, the easier it will be to target your offers, develop your copy and convert leads into actual sales.

Using your USP to Create a Benefits List

Once you have an idea what makes your company unique, you can start to message these differences as benefits to the customer.

While a lot of businesses get hung up on touting the features of their product or service, turning those features into benefits can be powerful in helping convert leads to sales.

The easiest way to turn a feature into a benefit is to look at all the features your product or service offers, and add a "…which means …" to the end.

For instance, if you're selling a high performance computer system with a million terabytes of storage and ten million megahertz of speed, you can create a sales benefit by saying, "…. which means you can store all the family videos and pictures you want on this machine, quickly and easily."

Simple scripts can be developed this way by listing all of the highlights and features of your products or services on one side of the page, separated by a "Which Means" heading, with benefits listed on the opposite side.

Benefits oriented selling helps open up rapport between your sales people and the leads coming in through your doors.

It can also help your average dollar sale because by showing extra value to your customers, you can charge more for the privilege of shopping with you.

Rapport is the first step to relationship, but you never get to the next step until you start a conversation built around what your company can do for your prospect or lead.

Your benefits list doesn't need to be long; maybe it's just three or four of the most important advantages your product or service will give your customers – aligned with the point of difference you are selling about your company, but just that little bit can be effective in many ways.

The Power and Effectiveness of Testimonials

If you don't have satisfied customers, it will be hard to get testimonials, but if you have a few raving fans, it won't be difficult.

So … start to gather them and use them in your sales pieces.

Why?

Testimonials are a great form of "word of mouth" advertising, and as you recall, word of mouth is the most effective (and lowest cost) marketing there is.

From a sales psychology standpoint, testimonials offer what is known as "social proof" … meaning that people are more likely to do things they know others they see as comparable to themselves are doing.

Testimonials can be used for any type of business.

In fact, one of the more successful case studies I've seen on the impact of testimonials was for a major business bank on the west coast.

After years of successfully using testimonials to drive their business, the executive team was tiring of the approach and wanted to move in a new and more "creative" direction.

(**Key Note:** Beware when your own team starts getting tired of advertising that works. Just because you've seen it for years, doesn't mean new prospects have, or that someone has finally decided to purchase from you based on that style of the campaign.)

Focus groups were convened and facilitated and paid for, feedback gathered, research conducted.

To their collective shock and surprise, the bank's best customers were actually upset the long-running campaign was going to be pulled.

Why?

To the person, they said they could relate to the people featured in the ads, and that the problems the people in the ads faced and overcame as the result of the bank's services were similar to those they faced … and needed to solve or overcome.

As a result, the bank continued the campaign for another five years, after which it was bought out by an even larger bank – that in turn completely switched its advertising to the working "template" that featured bank customers and their success stories with the organization.

Keys to Testimonials

The main key to successful testimonials is using customers and telling their stories.

Having a spokesperson or a "pitch" person isn't as effective, UNLESS it is the owner of the company … and then, it can be very effective (think back to Dave Thomas as the Wendy's spokesperson or Lee Iacocca back in the day as the then bankrupt Chrysler climbed back to respectability.)

The testimonials don't need to be fancy.

A simple quote, a full first and last name, and possibly a photo of the customers, is all you need to start the testimonial process ... and they can be included in your ads, brochures or online on your website, or on your blog or offline newsletter.

Video testimonials can be even more effective than written ones. In this day and age, people like watching videos and businesses shouldn't be afraid of taking advantage of that.

With reality television and social media, everyone has the ability to be noticed and it doesn't take a lot of money or even a lot of work.

Just use a handheld camera to videotape customers talking about your business or any special events that your business is involved with, then post them on your website.

Don't worry about production values.

Often, lesser production values in testimonials are a plus, not a minus, because it feels more "real" to the person watching.

There are even online sites that can house your testimonials like Angie's List.

Angie's List reviews thousands of businesses based on the opinions of real customers and there are no anonymous reviews.

There are even video libraries which house hundreds of testimonial videos.

If your business is competing with others for market share, a video testimonial on a site like Angie's List can be very helpful.

If you can create lots of video testimonials, go ahead and do it, you won't be sorry you did.

Testimonials are also a great way of showing customers that they weren't the first to buy a particular product, and that it's okay to say yes.

As with guarantees, testimonials help reassure people's decisions, which gives people a sense of certainty their decision to buy from you is the right one.

Offering a Private Label Brand or Exclusive Line of Products

Another effective way of converting leads and improving average dollar sale at the same time is to offer your own exclusive line of "Private Label" brands or products.

One really interesting example of this is a private label carried by Trader Joe's called Hofbrau beer.

If you've ever sampled one of Trader Joe's Hofbrau brews and found it suspiciously similar those beers found at the Gordon Biersch brewery chain of bars and restaurants, that's because they are brewed in the same Gordon Biersch facilities in San Jose.

The benefits for both are obvious, but this strategy isn't just limited to certain regions or products.

Big national retailers like Tesco in the UK offers a brand of petrol called President's Choice from the Canadian retailer Loblaw.

In the U.S., Costco has its own private label called Kirkland Signature, which offers everything from tires to fresh food and alcoholic beverages.

Whole Foods offers its "365 Everyday Value" line of products, which are both cost effective and high quality.

With almost 200 items, items in this line are among the bigger sellers for the company.

This type of strategy can also be very effective for professional service firms, where teams of lawyers create a brand alliance with a CPA firm, or marketing agencies create brand alliances with research or production companies.

Even if you charge less for exclusive items, it can help improve your average dollar sale because it may cost your business less to buy those items in the first place.

Differentiation Through Packaging or Design

You can also up your price points and the aesthetic value of your products by creating unique packaging or focusing on the design or layout of your retail outlet, or materials you present to customers.

In general, the better your packaging looks, the better chance you have of selling it, and this is especially true today with all of the products bought and sold on the internet.

Often customers never even see the product in real life, just through brochures or web pages.

Think about the times you've bought something online and received the package.

How did you feel when you received it?

Some companies make a big deal about their packaging, while others don't spend money on packaging because they feel they can save money.

Unfortunately those businesses are being penny-wise and pound-foolish.

Not only can packaging be a great way to make a first impression, it can be a great way to continue building the relationship with your customers and their lifetime value.

Of course, every company is different so the opposite can be true.

For natural or organic companies like "Burt's Bees," fancy packaging can be a negative because it wouldn't necessarily appeal to their clientele.

What really matters is that your packaging reflects your price point and appeals to your customers.

The one company that does this really well, of course, is Apple.

Everything from the Macbook to the iPod to the iPhone is sleekly and elegantly designed, packaged in simple and visually appealing boxes or containers, and equipped with easy to follow instruction booklets that are also in turn laid out in an appealing way.

Is there a correlation between Apple's commitment to aesthetic appeal and its cult-like following of literal lifetime customers?

I think so, and I also think you could make the case for aesthetic appeal for companies as diverse as Porsche and In-N-Out Burger, which presents its meals in a plain white box, hand wrapped in its signature "packaging."

Last I looked, In-N-Out continues to outpace a larger McDonald's in terms of same store sales and overall profits, not bad for a burger chain that only operates in a few states west of the Mississippi.

So, look at your packaging and design as a form of added value, and you can recover the costs with higher price points while upping your overall conversion rates.

And … who knows?

You can even make packaging so nice that, at some stage, it becomes a selling point unto itself.

For some people, just having a box from Tiffany's or some other high end store makes a difference in how they perceive and feel about themselves.

As long as your packaging represents your product, it can become a part of your overall product … to the point where your customers buy only on the basis of your name (which is the ultimate meaning of your "brand").

Offer Premium or Extremely High Quality Products

People will buy quality when it's affordable … and sometimes, even when it's not!

So if you offer premium or very high quality products, don't be afraid to adjust your price points accordingly.

People expect to pay more for quality and regard higher priced items as of a higher standard.

If you focus in a premium or high quality niche, be sure to have rigorous quality control checks, and even think about making that process a part of your overall sales messaging.

One company that does this well is BMW, which has touted itself as the "Ultimate Driving Machine" for more than four decades.

The company also promotes its service in its materials, and adds a free service component to its new car sales.

For that, BMW (like Apple) can continue to hold its price points and can use the free service as part of its initial sales process.

Offer Samples or Demonstrations

Samples and Demonstrations are also effective ways to eliminate risk for leads because it gives people an opportunity to experience how a product works or functions.

It also allows people to "sell themselves" based on how they process information.

What do I mean?

In general, people are oriented and process information three ways:

- Visually … meaning via sight
- Auditory … meaning via sound
- Kinesthetic … meaning via touch or feel

If you've ever taken a test drive for a new car, you'll immediately see why this is an important part of the buying process, as all senses are engaged with a test drive.

However, smart car sales people can leverage this process by getting clues about their buyers from things the buyers say or do.

Unique Demonstrations

How do you turn a networking event or bar fight into a demonstration?

It's easier than you think.

A car dealership hosted a fund-raiser and offered people test drives at the event with the idea that people would compare the car they just test drove with the car they would drive home.

Recently in New York, a vodka company tried a unique approach.

With permission, they hired actors to stage fake altercations that would stop just short of an actual fight.

Then, when the offending party admitted they were wrong, they would buy a round of that vodka for the entire bar.

They not only got attention at that moment, but gave people a story to tell anytime they ordered that vodka.

You can do this to … and adjust your one-on-one sales scripts to mirror and match your own potential buyers.

Here's how it works.

A car salesperson can pick up clues about a buyer's orientation within a few seconds after asking, "How can I help you?"

Answer:

"Just wanted to look at your new models …" (translation: Visually oriented)

"I've heard you have some good deals here …" (translation: Auditory oriented)

"I'm feeling like I want a new car and am interested in what you've got …" (translation: Kinesthetic oriented)

From there, the salesperson can guide the buyer with his or her own cues:

"Just look at this beautiful new model here …" (Visual)

"Just listen to this engine …" (Auditory)

> "Feel how comfortable the driver's seat is … as well as the back seat …" (Kinesthetic)

In a one-on-one sales process, you can come up with your own ways of positioning your "pitch" … but in large demonstrations or even workshops you can generally use these types of language to make sure you are hitting all of those types of people in your audience.

In general, most people are visuals, followed by auditory, followed by kinesthetic.

However, hitting all of your prospects' senses in this way will go far in helping you close more leads to sales.

Demonstrations as Networking Events

Sometimes when we think of demonstrations, we think simply in terms of TV pitch people selling their wares.

However, you can create the same type of experience (especially in a service or professional service business) by offering demonstrations as a group workshop, seminar, teaching or networking event.

This way, you are again looking to offer "value first" in offering your prospects a chance to deepen their knowledge, get in on the cutting edge of solving their problem, or having the secondary benefit of learning about your new product or service while connecting with others in their community or industry.

Increasing Conversions Online

Online, these conversion strategies can be easily adapted to your website or blog.

First off, you can use video links to offer yourself as a spokesperson or to show your product or service.

Video also allows you to speak directly to your customers so you can hit your message points.

You can also upload audio files onto your website, which can be used as an added value option for your blog (or even offline newsletter) … or positioned as instructional workshops for any of your product or service lines.

In general you want to keep your website or blog as simple as possible, and your cart system (if you have one) readily available.

You should also have the option of your potential (or current customers) being able to speak to a live person if they have questions about your site, or have trouble securing an order through your cart system.

This helps keep the connection with your leads and customers "live" … and offers evidence to your leads and customers that you truly are a customer service oriented organization.

Work ON It, Not IN It

Many in charge of businesses spend too much time working in it and not on it, but to produce truly spectacular results, this has to change.

Even those with a detailed understanding of business principles do it.

They find themselves operating on a specialist level rather than becoming a generalist and this can lead to trouble down the road.

When the person in charge is a specialist rather than a generalist they can lose sight of where they are heading and how to get there.

The business becomes like a rudderless ship, left to the will of the current.

A security company I worked with in Australia had this problem and it kept them from reaching the goals they'd set.

The owner was too busy in the day-to-day activities to find ways to grow and build his business.

He was putting his head down and working harder than ever and had no idea his business could even be improved.

After all, this particular business had been around since 1955, had a reputation for doing things a certain way, even if those ways weren't necessarily beneficial to the business.

They figured their performance was normal, and, sadly, it was.

It was the owner's fear of falling short of his retirement goals that got him to finally look for some help.

We set some goals and started improving the owner's education on what exactly he could do in his business to become profitable.

His goal was to improve his sales by 30% over the first 90 days through a more focused marketing plan and better scripting to improve his conversion rate.

Everything was tested and measured, so we knew what worked and what didn't.

We systemized simple routines, introduced scripts and installed a system to make processing job orders easier and to help information flow between departments.

We also worked out clear budgets and targets.

Making all of these changes wasn't easy.

A tight working culture and the routine of doing things the same way made it a challenge but changes needed to be made.

So what happened?

Over the first 90 days, this security company had increased their sales by 75%, well over the goal of 30% we had set.

Sales continued to climb thanks to a new focus on the customer and record sales were posted.

By the sixth month, this company had to hire a dedicated salesperson to handle all the leads they were getting.

By the end of the year, sales were up over 65 percent from the previous year and the company was operating in profit, rather than the loss they'd experienced in the past.

Now this business owner has time to focus on what really matters in life, his family and loved ones.

And it all happened because he started working ON his business and not IN it.

Chapter Review – "9 to Grow On"

1) A focus on Lifetime Value is customer service oriented, while a focus on Leads is marketing oriented. Focus on Conversion Rates means a focus on your sales and sales processes.

2) Having a guarantee is a great way to reduce your prospects' perceived risk of doing business with you. Some of the most successful companies in the world have been built by offering iron-clad guarantees.

3) You "Unique Selling Proposition," or USP, is also a key conversion point. People buy on points of difference, so it's important you know, tell and sell yours.

4) Testimonials are also a way to reduce perceived risk, and also offer "social proof" of the value of your company, products and services.

5) Offering a "private label" brand is another unique way to help convert leads into customers.

6) Differentiation on the basis of your packaging and design can not only be part of your USP strategy, it can be a selling point in itself.

7) Premium and/or high quality products or services can be another way to use your USP or point of difference to attract and convert a higher level of customer who will spend more over time with your company.

8) Samples and demonstrations are effective ways to present your product or service in a controlled and scripted way. You can also orient your scripts to appeal to the Visual, Auditory and Kinesthetic orientations of your prospects.

9) You can easily adopt and adapt any of these strategies in the online space, both with video, audio and easy-to-see or read testimonials and access to a cart system. Remember the human element counts online as well …and make sure there's always someone your prospects or customers can talk to if they have an issue or problem with your website.

3 Things to DO after your Review:

1) If don't have a guarantee, look at how you can develop one. If you do, see how you are currently positioning it to your prospects.

2) Take an inventory of items you see (or your customers see) as commodities. Can you create a private label brand and sell those at a premium? One good example is a Laundromat that repackaged inexpensive bleach and was able to sell it to those who customers who forgot it or who wanted it. With a catchy name and small, unique package, the owner was able to create a new and highly profitable volume of revenues.

3) What part of your business requires some extra explanation or "education" before prospects "get it" and become paying customers? Is there one? Can you find a way to turn this "problem" into a workshop or seminar opportunity ... that in turn helps convert them into customers?

Chapter 11:

Buying Customers Conclusion

We have covered a lot of ground in these pages, but one thing I hope you realize is that in today's business world, there is no "business as usual."

Companies simply can't waste resources to get new customers and not know what kind of return they are getting for their efforts.

My hope is that what we've covered will impress upon you the importance of a number of things that will literally allow you to profit in any company you may run, work in or produce systems to get more leads and more customers ...

1) Know your numbers.

You simply must know all of your numbers, and there's really no way around this if you want to profit and run a successful company.

Numbers are the language of business, and the best marketing, as we have seen, is simply math.

So start to learn and know and get comfortable in the numbers you need to learn and know to drive profits in your business.

And you can start with the "5 Ways." In reality, it is the only business formula you'll ever need to know.

2) Start seeing your customers as your best and biggest asset.

Nothing happens in business until a sale is made, and to truly profit in business, you need repeat business over time.

The only way to do this is with a good customer base, one that is attracted to your company because it wants to buy what you are selling, and you are selling what it wants to buy.

Once you start to see the long-term value of a profitable customer, you'll start to see and treat them as they are: just like gold.

3) Start buying profitable customers at a good price.

The whole concept of buying customers is a lot like value investing.

You're looking to pay a value price for an asset that will appreciate over time.

The great portfolio and investment manager Peter Lynch once called termed a stock that returned 15 times its initial investment a "fifteen bagger."

That's the type of ROI you want to shoot for in your own business.

The good news is, picking up a profitable new client or customers is a lot easier and less expensive than picking profitable stocks or shares.

4) Lifetime value equals repeat business. Repeat business equals profits.

The more transactions you can get from your customers over a longer length of time, the more profit you'll have and the more successful you'll be in business.

It's really as simple as that, and there are no real shortcuts other than knowing the numbers you need to get you there and the strategies you'll need to test and measure for your specific business.

5) Adopt the mindset that leads are more important than branding.

Stop the madness, the cost and the misinformation about "building a brand" or how to build a brand and focus instead on creating a systemized way to get qualified leads into your business ... while creating programs to keep your best customers and have them buy more from you.

6) Focus 80% of your efforts on your top 20% of your customers.

Once you eliminate 80% of your "C" and "D" customers, you'll have the energy and resources to focus 80% of your efforts on the top 20% of your customer base.

In the end, they will purchase more at higher prices over longer periods of time.

They will also be your best advocates by referring others like themselves to do business to you.

7) Have fun!

Business should be fun, and the best companies have distinct personalities and identities that draw and attract customers to them.

The best way to find ways to connect to your customers is to start to infuse your own personality and identity into your marketing (if you are the owner) ... or the personality and identity of your company (if you aren't the owner but are nevertheless looking to keep and get new customers for your company).

Having fun with your efforts will involve taking risks … and yes, in some cases will be uncomfortable.

However, the value you can create for your customers will be returned to you in the value they give back to your company by becoming customers for life.

I hope you've found all of this valuable in its own right, and I know that by using and implementing what we've covered, you'll develop your own business wisdom that will allow you to continually buy customers at a great price.

I also know when you get to that point, you'll always be able to buy the customers you want … whenever and wherever you are, to build the great company you deserve.

Glossary

A, B, C and D Customers: An easy way to segment a company's customer base. There are four categories of customers:

1.   A Customers are Awesome.

2.   B Customers are Basic.

3.   C Customers are ones you "Can't deal with."

4.   D Customers are to be considered "Dead" to your business.

AIDA ("Attention-Interest-Desire-Action"): The conventional advertising "formula" that states effective ads need to generate "Attention, Interest, Desire and Action." A more focused way to help boost AIDA is with the additional formula "Target, Offer and Copy."

Buying Customers: A "new" way to look at getting new customers into a business. It is simply looking to buy the best customer at the lowest possible price for the longest amount of time with a number of tested and measured strategies.

Blog: A "weblog." For the purposes of business, a business "diary" or communication on a dedicated URL or web site that is updated with content, video or links that is intended to communicate with a customer base.

Branding: A long-term and expensive form of marketing and advertising that seeks to cause or persuade customers to buy solely on the basis of a name, trademark or logo.

Closed Door Sales: Closed Door Sales are normally special invitation events that are only open to a company's A and B customers.

Conversion Rates: The rate or percentage of the leads your company converts to an actual sale. Simply divide your sales by your number of leads to get this number. Multiply by 100 to get a percentage.

For example:

Your Sales / Total Number of Leads X 100= Your Conversion Rate

50 Sales / 1000 leads = .05 X 100 = 5% Conversion Rate

Cycle of Business: A different way of looking at your company, where the owner supports the team, the team supports the customers, the customers support the business, and finally, the business supports the owner.

The "5 Ways" Formula: The "5 Ways" Formula is a formula that focuses on 5 key profit drivers that exist in any business.

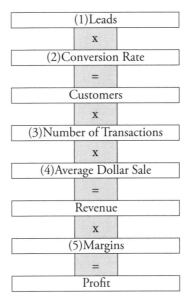

| (1)Leads |
| X |
| (2)Conversion Rate |
| = |
| Customers |
| X |
| (3)Number of Transactions |
| X |
| (4)Average Dollar Sale |
| = |
| Revenue |
| X |
| (5)Margins |
| = |
| Profit |

Lead: A person who expresses an interest, inquires, or requests information about your business.

Lead Generation: The first of the "5 Ways" strategies that focus on generating more leads. Most companies focus on this strategy first, not realizing it is the most expensive (and for most companies) least effective ways to get new customers.

Lifetime Value: Essentially, repeat business, or the amount of repeat business or business transactions an average customer will transact over the course of the customer's relationship with the business.

To quantify Lifetime Value, you can estimate by plugging numbers into the formula:

Average Value of a Sale X Number of Repeat Transactions X Average Retention Time (in Months or Years) of a Typical Customer

For example, the Lifetime Value of a gym member who spends $20 per month, every month, for 3 years, would be:

$20 X 12 months X 3 years.
= $240 X 3 = $720

Niche: "A place, employment, status, or activity for which a person or thing is best fitted." It's also defined as a "specialized market."

Either way, finding and focusing on your niche is the most powerful way to leverage all the resources and activities in a business.

9 Basic Needs of the Customer: Basic human needs that if met, can help drive your customers service programs. They are:

1) Subsistence

2) Protection

3) Affection

4) Understanding

5) Participation

6) Leisure

7) Creation

8) Identity

9) Freedom

The Pareto Principle: Also known as the "80/20 rule," the Pareto Principle means that in most companies, 80% of all revenues comes from 20% of your top customers.

Perceived Value Offers: Any offer that gives value other than quantifiable results. One way to up perceived value is to place limits on offers, making them more "scare" or "rare." This could be a "limited time" offer, or an exclusive offer of limited quantity items or services.

Raving Fans: These are your company's best advocates. They are customers who recommend you to their networks, families and friends. Creating Raving Fans should be the goal of every company, as their "word-of-mouth" advertising for your business is the lowest cost and most effective advertising you can have.

6 Keys to a Winning Team: There are six keys that go into building a great team.

1.   Strong Leadership
2.   A Common Goal
3.   Rules of the Game
4.   An Action Plan
5.   Company Support in Risk Taking and …
6.   100 Percent Involvement and Inclusion

"Target, Offer, Copy:" An alternative advertising formula focused on narrowing down a company's audience, creating a compelling offer, and orienting copy or message points around that offer. It borrows from and adds to the direct response formula that states the two most important parts of any direct marketing campaign are a quality (or qualified) data base and the offer to that data base.

Contact Details

AMERICAS
5781 S. Fort Apache
Las Vegas, NV 89148
United States
phone: +1 702-795-3188
fax: +1 702-795-3183
www.actioncoach.com

ASIA PACIFIC
1/44 Borthwick Avenue
Murrarrie QLD 4172
Ph: +61 7 3900 5500
australia@actioncoach.com

LATIN AMERICA
Ricardo Margain 201-19
Plaza Santa Engracia
Colonia Santa Engracia Garza Garcia
Nuevo Leon 66267 Mexico
Ph: +52 818 335 8194
mex@actioncoach.com

Twitter
Twitter.com/ActionCOACH

Facebook
www.facebook.com/ActionCOACHBusinessCoaching

Brad Sugars' website
www.bradsugars.com

Here's how you can profit from all of Brad's ideas with your local **ActionCOACH** Business Coach

Just like a sporting coach pushes an athlete to achieve optimum performance, provides them with support when they are exhausted, and teaches the athlete to execute plays that the competition does not anticipate.

A business coach will make you run more laps than you feel like. A business coach will show it like it is. And a business coach will listen.

The role of an **ActionCOACH** Business Coach is to show you how to improve your business through guidance, support, and encouragement. Your coach will help you with your sales, marketing, management, team building, and so much more. Just like a sporting coach, your **ActionCOACH** Business Coach will help you and your business perform at levels you never thought possible.

Whether you've been in business for a week or 20 years, it's the right time to meet with and see how you'll profit from an **ActionCOACH.**

As the owner of a business it's hard enough to keep pace with all the changes and innovations going on in your industry, let alone to find the time to devote to sales, marketing, systems, planning and team management, and then to run your business as well.

As the world of business moves faster and becomes more competitive, having a Business Coach is no longer a luxury; it has become a necessity. Based on the sales, marketing, and business management systems created by Brad Sugars, your **ActionCOACH** is trained to not only show you how to increase your business revenues and profits but also how to develop your business so that you, as the owner, can take back control. All with the aim of your working less and relaxing more. Making money is one thing; having the time to enjoy it is another.

Your **ActionCOACH** Business Coach will become your marketing manager, your sales director, your training coordinator, your confidant, your mentor. In short, your **ActionCOACH** will help you make your business dreams come true.

ATTENTION BUSINESS OWNERS
You can increase your profits now!

Here's how you can have one of Brad's **ActionCOACH** Business Coaches guide you to success.

Like every successful sporting icon or team, a business needs a coach to help it achieve its full potential. In order to guarantee your business success, you can have one of Brad's team as your business coach. You will learn about how you can get amazing results with the help of the team at **ActionCOACH**.

The business coaches are ready to take you and your business on a journey that will reward you for the rest of your life. You see, we believe **ActionCOACH** speaks louder than words.

Visit lasvegas@actioncoach.com, or fill out and fax this card to your local **ActionCOACH** office to discover how our team can help you increase your income today!

ActionCOACH
The World's Number-1 Business Coaching Team

Name...

Position..

Company...

Address ....

Country...

Phone...

Fax..

Email..

Referred by..

How do I become an **ActionCOACH** Business Coach?

If you choose to invest your time and money in a great business and you're looking for a white-collar franchise opportunity to build yourself a lifestyle, an income, a way to take control of your life and , a way to get great personal satisfaction...

Then you've just found the world's best team!

Now, it's about finding out if you've got what it takes to really enjoy and thrive in this amazing business opportunity.

Here are the 4 things we look for in every **ActionCOACH**:

1. You've got to love succeeding

We're looking for people who love success, who love getting out there and making things happen. People who enjoy mixing with other people, people who thrive on learning and growing, and people who want to charge an hourly rate most professionals only dream of.

2. You've got to love being in charge of your own life

When you're ready to take control, the key is to be in business for yourself, but not by yourself. **ActionCOACH's** support, our training, our world leading systems, and the backup of a global team are all waiting to give you the best chance of being an amazing business success.

3. You've got to love helping people

Being a great Coach is all about helping yourself by helping others. The first time clients thank you for showing them step by step how to make more money and work less within their business, will be the day you realize just how great being an Action Business Coach really is.

4. You've got to love a great lifestyle

Working from home, setting your own timetable, spending time with family and friends, knowing that the hard work you do is for your own company and, not having to climb a so-called corporate ladder. This is what lifestyle is all about. Remember, business is supposed to give you a life, not take it away.

Our business is booming and we're seriously looking for people ready to find out more about how becoming a member of the **ActionCOACH** Business Coaching team is going to be the best decision you've ever made.

Apply online now at **www.actioncoach.com**

Here's how you can network, get new leads, build yourself an instant sales team, learn, grow and build a great team of supportive business owners around you by checking into your local ActionCOACH's ProfitCLUB.

Joining your local ActionCOACH's ProfitCLUB is about more than just networking, it's also the learning and exchanging of profitable ideas.

Embark on a journey to a more profitable enterprise by meeting with fellow, like-minded business owners.

An **ActionCOACH's** ProfitCLUB is an excellent way to network with business people and business owners. You will meet every two weeks for breakfast to network and learn profitable strategies to grow your business.

Here are three reasons why **ActionCOACH's** ProfitCLUB work where other networking groups don't:

1. You know networking is a great idea. The challenge is find the time and maintaining the motivation to keep it up and make it a part of your business. If you're not really having fun and getting the benefits, you'll find it gets easier to find excuses that stop you going. So, we guarantee you will always have fun and learn a lot from bi-weekly group meetings.

2. The real problem is that so few people do any work 'on' their business. Instead they generally work "in" it, until it's too late. By being a member of an **ActionCOACH's** ProfitCLUB, you get to attend FREE business-building workshops run by Business Coaches that teach you how to work "on" your business and avoid this common pitfall and help you to grow your business

3. Unlike other groups, we have marketing systems to assist in your groups' growth rather than just relying on you to bring in new members. This way you can concentrate on YOUR business rather than on ours.

Latest statistics show that the average person knows at least 200 other contacts. By being a member of your local **ActionCOACH's** ProfitCLUB, you have an instant network of around 3,000 people.

Join your local **ActionCOACH's** ProfitCLUB today.

Apply online now at **www.actioncoach.com**

Leverage-The Game of Business

You Business Success is just a Few Games Away

Leverage - The Game of Business is a fun way to learn how to succeed in business fast. The rewards start slowing the moment you start plating!

Leverage is three hours of fun, learning, and discovering how you can be an amazingly successful business person.

It's a breakthrough in education that will have you racking up the profits in no time. The principles you take away from playing this game will set you up for a life of business success. It will open your mind to what's truly possible. Apply what you learn and sit back and watch your profits soar.

By playing this fun and interactive business game, you will learn:

* How to quickly raise business income
* How business people can become rich and successful in a short space of time
* How to create a business that works without you

Isn't it time you had the edge over your competition?

Leverage has been played by all age groups from 12-85 and has been a huge learning experience for all. The most common comment we hear is: "I thought I knew a lot, and just by playing a simple board game I have realized I have a long way to go. The knowledge I've gained from playing Leverage will make me thousands! Thanks for the lesson."

For ordering information, call 888-483-2828